DIGITAL RETAIL MARKETING

DIGITAL RETAIL MARKETING

The Essential Guide to Low-Cost Successful Content Marketing

DARIO SIPOS

Published in the European Union by DWR Ltd.
(*www.dwr-eu.eu*)

ISBN 978-953-49031-0-0 (paperback)
ISBN 978-953-49031-1-7 (eBook)
ISBN 978-953-49031-2-4 (audiobook)

Table of Contents

Dario Sipos is a digital marketing strategist, branding expert, keynote public speaker, author, and business columnist. He has built his unique skill set during 10+ years of experience working in every aspect of digital marketing. He has spent significant time working all over the world in the digital field, helping clients, and developing brands.

When you gain online influence, you have the ability to transform minds, behaviors, and outcomes. Dario will help you become an influential presence on the Internet, which means that people will respect your opinions, trust your judgment, and listen to your voice above all others.

Dario helps leaders influence positive outcomes in all directions, even under the most difficult and changing conditions.

To find out more about Dario and his journey, follow him at:

www.dariosipos.com

THE FUTURE OF ADVERTISING – ADS ARE SUFFOCATING THE WEB

My children tell me that inventing a banner ad is like inventing smallpox.

J.McCambley (inventor of the banner ad)

HOW MANY PEOPLE WOKE UP this morning saying: "I so wish I could see an advertisement right now?"

Probably none, but why, then, do marketing staff go to work and say: "Let's make another advertisement."

Ten years ago, idealists were speaking about the "fight against the machine" and saying the "web needs to remain free." But it seems that battle is over because distracting pop-ups and animated advertisements are everywhere.

For almost twenty years, the digital advertising industry has displayed symptoms of sociopathic behavior: spreading ruthlessly, without care for users; undermining the basic purpose of business, to be useful to customers; and making mad anyone in its path.

Different standards of viewability create ads that are impossible to view, or that make it impossible for people to see anything other than the ads. Ads are suffocating the web.

The two most significant issues facing the advertising industry currently are ad blocking and advertising monopolies. Ad blocking is just a reflex of an audience growing disgusted with an industry that shows almost no regard for peoples' needs and desires. The second issue is the fact that network effects tend to create only monopolies. The advertisement industry depends mostly on the two largest: Facebook and Google. Their combined share of online Ad budgets ranges from 60 to 75%.

Monopole behavior is only going to get more dramatic. Reports show that both Facebook and Google repeatedly manage to grab three-quarters of all growth in digital advertising. Monopolies, even when divided between two companies, do not support competition, transparency, and innovation.

THE GOOD OLD DAYS OF MARKETING

This terrible situation that we're in now, where audiences are continuously bombarded with ads, drives retailers' fears of change and their dedicated devotion to the good old days of traditional marketing.

Retailers, dedicated to keeping alive the glory of the good old days, fail to understand the complexity of digital marketing, and how it differs from leaflets, TV, large posters, and others. They also fail to understand how real people consume digital forms of marketing.

This issue derives from retailers not knowing the technical complexity of buying digital media space to actually place an advertisement on the web, the limitations of retargeting, the technological possibilities of ad-serving platforms, and not knowing about users defended privacy and security.

Agencies and brands also fail to see that digital marketing requires a creative approach that is the opposite of the conventional approach used to write sales messages for traditional ads. A lack of creative approach becomes apparent, for example, when a retailer develops their own-brand products and doesn't manage to distinguish them in a sea of other similar products.

When brands on the web ask users "how can we help you?", instead of "what can we sell to you?" then they will see victory. However, most retailers do not know how to be helpful online and merely rely on passive communication with existing customers.

Content marketers are leading the attack on online ads, since the first banners appeared, pushing the idea that the only meaningful way for brands to use the web is to provide valuable, useful content to users. This fundamental good idea became corrupted as soon as big advertising stepped into the picture.

After some time, useful content was replaced by measures which only big traditional marketing agencies understand: reach and frequency. They pushed out the same ads that had been on TV and printed media for decades: good old-fashioned sales messages.

If ads worked on the Internet, then ad blockers would not have been made. All media is becoming digital, not just ads, which tells us there will be nowhere else for advertising to go.

Where will ads go once all media has moved to digital? The ads industry has failed to answer this question for the last two decades. By failing to address the issue, they created opportunities for content marketers, who own the only solution for marketing's future.

Steps towards Digital Dignity and Progress

Content marketing provides a guaranteed approach to transform commercials to content that is valued by internet users, which attracts their attention, and works with different digital platforms.

The long-made promise of internet ads as a low-cost and reliable source of influence on the public has failed.

Despite the fact that users are apparently frustrated by the current system of online ads, there is no evident desire for change in the retail marketing industry. Marketing creators should realize that the *quality* of promotional material is more important than the *quantity*.

If you wish to step into the future of advertising and stop suffocating the web with ads for your retail business, this book will help you in that endeavor.

The most crucial step is to hand over your marketing and advertising activities to content marketers; they will find a way to provide value to people through marketing messages.

Digital agencies mostly do what clients demand from them: All the continued unsound practices are generated by clients who put money behind their insistent requests. Only the company or brand itself can properly plan, create, and execute a digital awareness campaign because they understand their industry, product, and customers better than an outsourced digital agency does. To simplify, we can say that a digital agency is only as good as their client is, meaning that the agency can only perform to the standard dictated by the client. The more a client knows about content marketing and brand building online then, as a result, the digital agency will be more successful in promoting the client online.

DIGITAL-FIRST APPROACH

Be aware that people do not wake up in the morning with the desire to see your ads. It's a good idea not to interrupt users from what they were doing on the Internet with your ads.

In this book, you will learn to take critical steps to stop irritating people with your internet ads by avoiding, for example, unnecessary and distracting animations and flashy promises. Before doing any marketing, you should always ask yourself and your team if there is a better way to attract the attention of your target audience?

As part of this process, you will have to make organizational changes to integrate all your marketing efforts while implementing the digital-first approach.

Simply repeating your TV commercials or leaflets in a digital format online is a suicidal move. Playing your latest TV commercial on your company web page is not going to work. The organizational transformation will be simple, but not easy to achieve.

CREATING VALUABLE AND USEFUL CONTENT

The most significant change in approach will come from carefully deciding what type of content to create. Stories about yourself or your latest achievements in sales will not be enough for success. The audience has the power to block such content. The idea behind the web a few decades ago was to make communication easier.

Asking yourself, "how can we help people?" developed on the real examples of your company helping people is the route to success.

Giving people repetitive sales messages is not going to work because digital media is different from traditional media. The idea behind ads is to provide earnings for publishers and advertisers, while the publisher's goals are not to provide excellent user experience but to solely increase earnings. People can prevent the display of such ads.

If retailers do not start providing useful content, instead of ads, there will be fewer and fewer customers. Soon ads should become less suffocating and smarter. In case they do not, there is always an adblocker.

Chapter 1

RETAIL MARKETING IN A DIGITAL AGE

Content Marketing is all the Marketing that's left.

Seth Godin

THE PURPOSE OF THIS BOOK is to demonstrate and teach you the most effective digital content marketing strategy for a retail business, by which you will grow your business and brand in a simple process.

That process will be low-cost, compared to classical marketing methods, while relying on your ingenuity, consistency, and team resources. The process eliminates the need for beautifully designed content by expensive outsourced marketing agencies, which is the most popular resort for so many retailers when trying to start their content marketing journey.

By successfully going through the complete book, you will:

1. Have a systematic knowledge about the content marketing process, story branding, useful tools, and how all parts come together to work as a productive machine.
2. Understand the psychology behind acquiring users online and how social media algorithms work.
3. Know how successful content marketing grows your retail brand while keeping costs low.
4. Be entirely ready and capable to start and continuously run your retail content marketing process.

At the following link: *www.dariosipos.com/resources* you can download for free the extra content associated with this book in the form of infographics and other useful data.

Chapter 11 of this book is a step-by-step guide to establish proper content marketing transformation in retail. This chapter was created by drawing on successful experiences of a dozen small–large-sized European retailers and one South African large-sized retailer. The beauty of the process described in chapter 11 is that it proved to be successful in any size company, throughout various cultures and vast geographical territories. Even though the original intention of the process described in chapter 11 was to help in retail marketing, it will also prove useful in creating and marketing own-brand labels and wholesale expansion.

Before you dive into the exact steps to transform your retail content marketing efforts, it is crucial that you understand the concepts described in all the following chapters.

Definition of Retail

According to the most common definition, **retail** is the sale of various goods and services to customers with the intention of making a profit.

Retail includes selling through various channels, so sales made online and those made in-store both apply.

Some companies are exceptionally good at online sales and, for a brief moment, the world was convinced that online sales would win over offline sales. The truth is somewhere in the middle, so both types of sales matter and companies capable of doing both will most likely survive the future with more profits.

Omnichannel is defined as the multichannel sales approach that provides the customer with a combined shopping experience. The customer can be shopping online from a desktop or mobile device, via phone, or in a brick and mortar store, and the experience will be flawless.

A Brief History of Retail Stores

The first retail stores were developed by 800 BC in ancient Greece, where society had developed markets with merchants selling goods.

To jump forward to our times, in the period from 1700 to 1800, plenty of "mom and pop" stores were developed, especially throughout the United States. "Mom and pop" is a colloquial phrase for a small business owned by a family.

In the mid-1800s and early 1900s, department stores were created to satisfy the broader tastes of consumers. The first department stores, Macy's (1858), Bloomingdales (1861), and Sears (1886), became influencers because they were directly able to impact what people bought, how they organized their homes, and what products they thought were needed. Stores actively provided demonstrations of products and entertainment events that convinced customers to spend more of their income.

Shopping malls started appearing in the 1950s, although the first outdoor shopping plaza opened in 1922 in Kansas City. The first indoor shopping mall, similar to today's concept of the shopping mall, was opened in 1956 in Edina, Minnesota.

With e-commerce sales growing, the appeal of malls has steadily declined, hitting a twenty-year low by the end of 2019.

Today consumers are actively looking for majestic experiences, and rich content as part of their shopping activities, which can influence what they buy. In the Digital Age, brands are finding out that building strong content and experience-led shopping can affect their sales and profits significantly.

New Opportunities in Retail Business

Noticeably one of the most significant landmarks in the history of retail is the appearance of internet shopping. As evident worldwide, in the last three decades, consumers are excited to use e-commerce.

The reason for this excitement and loyalty is that e-commerce provides convenience; a shopper can research products, compare prices, and purchase at any time of the day.

Since 2007, new opportunities for retail appeared after social networks were brought to life. Social media is an excellent opportunity for any retailer, but also a massive challenge for retailers that attempt to conquer them.

In only a decade, e-commerce has grown from 5% of the retail market to nearly 15%.

Customers desire online shopping experiences, so successful brands are developing a string of multi-channel strategies.

CONTENT MARKETING IN RETAIL

Content marketing is a well-thought-out marketing tool focused on creating and delivering valuable, relevant content designed to attract and engage a clearly-defined audience – and drive them to do business with you.

Retail Content marketing helps to build loyalty with customers that will last for decades.

Content marketing in retail is not a new thing, but its popularity grew in recent decades with the rise of the Internet.

Previously, the methods of marketing used for decades hadn't changed much: TV, printing leaflets, brochures, and catalogs. These methods are now being won over by companies creating engaging content.

Why did that happen? Why has creating engaging content online suddenly became so crucial for your retail business? The answer is that consumers moved their life and now search for interests online, forming a new relationship between customers and retail stores.

Overcoming the ingrained practice of only working with traditional marketing methods, which no longer work as in the past, has become a challenging task within the retail industry.

Simply, the medium has evolved over time, but the structure and system for creating successful content in the retail business are pretty much the same.

Content marketing in retail is about:
* What your customers value
* Their life aspirations
* How your business helps them achieve their goals
* How you can help customers by providing value, educating them, and also entertaining them

Growth of your online sales is all about the audience and creating trust between you and them. Once trust is established you are more likely to sell the products you offer to those customers.

The process of enabling customers to find you online is a result of steady, consistent work. The process itself requires a lot of consistency, which is the part where most retailers fall down. Customers can only find you online if you publish content online.

Content marketing costs significantly less than traditional marketing in retail. Content marketing, at the same time, provides easily documented and considerably higher results.

The point of content is that it creates a flow in the customer's mind, on a path to convince them to trust you and eventually make a purchase.

At the same time, your content has the intention of bringing a particular type of person to your e-commerce site and helping them make a purchase.

The ultimate goal is to turn customers into "brand ambassadors" that will spread positive messages through word-of-mouth and direct more people to your business.

Instead of notifying customers about your products and services with leaflets and catalogs, you should create content that your current and future customers will love and engage with. Engaging content will build a long-lasting relationship between the customer and your retail.

The less you know or the fewer methods you use in your e-commerce journey, the more you are limiting yourself and the growth of your business.

By the end of this book, you will become an expert at retail content marketing. Additionally, you should also study all other aspects of e-commerce that can push that process forward and influence your online success positively.

At the following link, you can download an infographic showing all aspects of a successful e-commerce store: *www.dariosipos.com/resources.*

As we progress through the chapters, all the subjects involved in digital marketing for retail will become clear. Let's dive into content marketing for retail.

Chapter 2

THE REALITY OF ONLINE MARKETING

A brand is a customer experience represented by a collection of marketing ideas and information; often, it refers to a symbol such as a name, logo, slogan, and design scheme. Brand recognition and other reactions are created by the accumulation of experiences with the specific product or service, both directly relating to its use, and through the influence of advertising, design, and media commentary.

Dictionary of Marketing Terms,
American Marketing Association (AMA), 2015

BRAND APPEARANCE ONLINE

WHAT CONSTITUTES A BRAND IS a matter of perception, and you know if some branding is working when you see that brand around you.

Branding these days is happening in the time when more and more people are moving to the Internet, or they are already on the Internet. As all events on the Internet happen rapidly brands can be created online very quickly, or destroyed quickly too.

More importantly, it means that your brand can be steadily built up over time while reaching far more people on a lower budget than before.

A considerable advantage is that smaller retailers can reach more people than ever before. Still, to do it right, it is not just a matter of being on top of search engines, but it's also a matter of being different from competitors in a positive way.

Companies can use their brands as a management tool to motivate and guide employees, win customers, align activities, and communicate with core brand messages. A successful brand has an uplifting, energizing power.

Great brands will connect their internal culture to a larger movement to establish relevance and emotional connection.

A brand is not an image of a company; a brand is what the company does, which means that brands are about actions they take instead of advertising.

The real differentiator of a successful brand is a consistent look and feel online.

When you see a real brand online, it will have many media types and channels where customers and prospects can communicate with them (blogs, Facebook, Twitter, Pinterest, YouTube, Instagram, brand website, and potentially many others). All those media types and channels will always be used by brands to showcase the values they want to represent to the public.

As the Internet is an enormous space, to be seen or heard your brand needs to have a clear **value proposition**. In other words, what do you offer the audience that is attractive to them, that adds value to their experience? Perhaps you offer great online support which is fast and efficient, free returns, or fast delivery. But just repeating these facts to customers on your social media pages isn't enough to make those pages attractive; they need to be wrapped in entertaining content so the audience actually wants to visit and engage with you.

Psychology of Customers Online

Marketing manuals and handbooks are, in most cases, not valid anymore. While you follow known promotion rules, competition is bypassing them by creating their own rules and pushing it to the public using creative marketing methods.

Peoples' habits are changing online, and new habits are silencing traditional marketing tactics.

Customers and prospects are getting better at blocking non-desired messages: Calls can be blocked, emails sent to spam, TV commercials skipped, and the list of evasion methods becomes bigger every day.

At the same time, your competitor probably has a massive marketing budget, and they are not afraid to use it against you.

When you pay for ads, you are not really buying attention, you are just renting it for a short time because ads are temporary. When you stop paying the rent, you stop getting attention.

Online, finding customers means that you need to become what customers *want* to consume. So instead of finding customers, they will find you.

Therefore, your content marketing efforts online should be about outsmarting the competition, instead of outspending them. It is about providing hooks to customers that will make them desire to return to you.

It is about providing customers something that they will appreciate, and that will have value for them.

Classical retail marketing is mostly not well regarded online because it is often described as: Loud, interruptive, insensitive, annoying, impersonal, and ignorant

Content retail marketing is well-accepted online because it is often described as: Personal, valuable, meaningful, engaging, respectful, informative, endearing, lovable, and insightful

THE HOOK MODEL: BUILDING A HABIT

The ultimate retailer goal is to make consumers incorporate your products and services into their daily routines, to the level that it becomes a habit.

The definition of a **habit** is behavior that is done without too much thinking.

Social media has habit-forming potential, which is one of the aspects of their digital innovation, next to constant availability for communication.

Consumer psychologist Nir Eyal developed the "Hook Model" in his book *Hooked*. He created his four-step model by researching common traits between successful products, using insights from behavioral psychology and neuroscience, and combining it with his personal experience in the advertising industry.

The Hook is a process that companies use to "catch" consumers, so dealing with your business will become a habit for them. Such consumers will also become your brand ambassadors that will bring new users by word-of-mouth at little or no cost at all.

THE HOOK MODEL

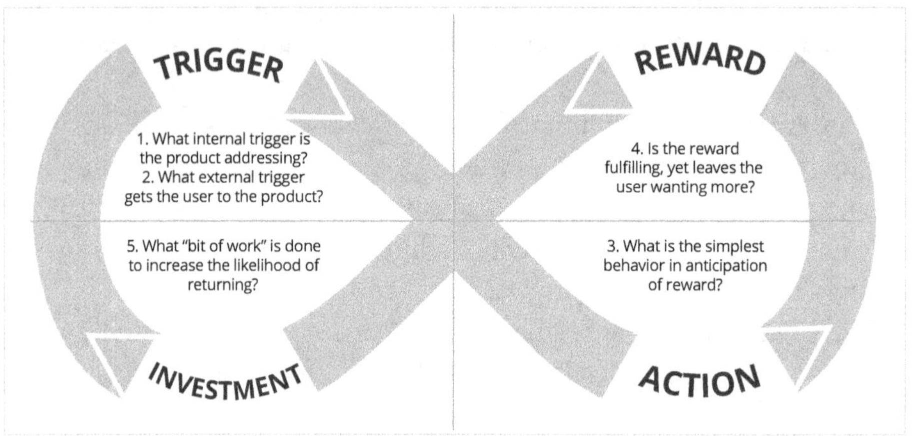

Figure 1. The Hook Model
Source: *Hooked*, Nir Eyal

The four stages of the Hook model are: trigger, action, variable reward, investment.

There are external and internal triggers which cause people to carry out the desired action, and that action happens because people expect rewards.

External triggers are the ones where information about what to do next is within the trigger (emails, billboards, other).

Internal triggers are the ones where the information for what to do next is formed through an association in the user's memory (people, places, emotions, situations, routines).

People are more likely to develop such habits when they have to invest some time in going through the hook process, because this forms the internal triggers and creates the impression that their work resulted in a reward. For many, and especially the younger generations, posting content on social media networks and receiving engagement from others is equal to real work in the real world.

Successful businesses solve peoples' pain by formulating products and services as relief from pain points.

When a company manages to make an offer that forms a habit, the competition will struggle to break through that barrier even with a much superior product.

All retailers can use the Hook model to get consumers on board with their service and products. Once consumers are hooked, there is less need for marketing and advertising. Hooked consumers will advertise your business online by word-of-mouth.

There is no hook for customers or prospects in paid ads. The only people who are hooked by paid ads are the CEOs and marketing managers who paid for them. When they see their company or brand pop up in a paid ad, they feel rewarded and want to see more. So, they pay for more ads. They're hooked!

The steps in the Hook model, seen in the above diagram, are detailed below:

1. **Trigger: The Activator of Behavior**

Either external or internal, both are signs telling people what action they should take.

When a person sees an external trigger, it will direct them to a particular action (for example, a login button on a web page is an online trigger).

External triggers can be one of four categories:
* **Earned** – Publicizing an event or creating a video with the hope of becoming viral.
* **Paid** – Buying advertising space to attract new users and convert them into loyal customers.
* **Relationship** – Such as word-of-mouth recommendations via social media, user forums, or other digital communication methods.
* **Owned** – After receiving users' permission, the company can push notifications to users. For example, to the smartphone of the user or their web-browser.

Internal triggers are subconscious associations between emotion and action or thought. For example, boredom will often drive you to check your email. People will often form habitual reactions to some experiences or pain points during their day. Businesses exploit users' pain points by offering comfort or solutions to their problems.

Businesses will greatly benefit if they can understand which internal triggers cause people to use their products or services.

2. **Action: Anticipation of a Reward**

Action is what a trigger is trying to spark. When people act by habit, they act instinctively with almost no thought about it. In this case, action is how you behave because you expect a reward.

The actions that require little mental effort form habits. Social networks use a model where they identify human desires; usually the ones that exist for a long time, and then use steps of hooking to create a habit. Searching on Google doesn't take a lot of time or effort, so it becomes a habit for human beings to use it often.

3. **Variable Reward: Creating Craving**

The Hook model builds desire by creating cravings. When people act, they experience the relief of solving their problem or satisfying their urge. Giving users variable instead of full rewards will create more needs.

Studies of reward mechanism behavior show that anticipation of a reward activates the brain's pleasure center. At the same time when people expect rewards, incentives start becoming less attractive. Introducing variable, unexpected, or intermittent rewards revives activity in the brain's pleasure center.

Variable rewards belong to one of the following types: the tribe, the hunt, and the self. Tribe rewards tap into the desire to connect socially and to feel included. Social media sites and computer games exploit this universal craving. People visit social media repeatedly to see if their friends "like" their posts. Games give users the chance to earn different types of badges in recognition of their achievements.

4. **Investment: The User Does Some Work**

When people invest more effort in their purchase, they become more committed, and even small investments of time or energy create bonds. For example, part of the appeal of IKEA is that they need to invest effort in assembling furniture, compared to when they purchase ready-made furniture. In the most cases the effort is minimal, and the price reflects the fact that customers have to do some of the work themselves.

When people commit to behavior, it is highly likely they will repeat it in the future, if the reward is naturally positive.

For example, when users post their resumes on LinkedIn and use the time to add data to their profiles, it is unlikely they will switch to another similar site and repeat the sign-up process again.

The Hook model is circular because external triggers encourage users to return, making their habits stronger each time.

Social Media sites are habits that most people use daily, precisely as their designers intended.

Chapter 3

INTERNET TRAFFIC AND ALGORITHMS

Google only loves you when everyone else loves you first.
Wendy Piersall

TYPES OF INTERNET TRAFFIC

ORGANIC TRAFFIC IS THE TERM used to describe visits to a website coming from a search engine's organic results and not from paid ads.

After users enter a query in a search engine (such as Google or Bing), they are presented with a set of results that include both the pages ranking on the top positions organically and a set of ads (usually denoted with the word "Ad") to differentiate them from the organic results.

After a user clicks on organic search results leading them to a website, then that action is recorded in an analytic tool as organic search traffic.

The most crucial difference in comparing paid to organic traffic is that the former is paid, and the latter is free.

There are two ways to get traffic from search engines. Your website can be ranked high in the search results, or you could pay an ads service (such as Google Ads) to place your ads on top of the organic results with advertising.

With organic traffic, you can get visits to your website as long as you rank high enough that users will see your site on search engine results pages. On the other hand, with paid traffic, visits will drop as soon as you stop paying for ads. Therefore, by paying for ads, you are just temporarily renting attention. Whereas with organic efforts, you create permanent results in search engine rankings.

Most companies are focused on getting paid traffic at a high cost, instead of focusing on getting organic traffic with no cost or little cost to generate it (in most cases, just the cost of the workforce generating organic traffic).

Building organic traffic takes a longer time, but it is free and works at any time, while with paid traffic, you will get quick results but will also have to pay each time someone visits your site.

If you are not at the top of search engine results, then customers will not find you. Your first customer is actually a search engine, and you need to convince it that your business deserves a top position in search engine results.

Organic traffic is the most essential traffic that you can get to your website, with the simple reason that organic traffic is targeted. When people type a query in a search engine, they have a specific intent, and if you can provide them a solution, then you might gain a new customer.

Possible traffic sources to your website include:

* Organic traffic – Traffic from search engines' organic results and not paid ads
* Paid search – Traffic to a website from paid ads
* Direct traffic – Traffic to a website when users directly type your URL in the browser
* Referral traffic – Traffic from a click on another website that leads them to your website
* Social traffic – Traffic coming from social media networks (Twitter, Facebook, LinkedIn, Pinterest, and others)
* Display – Traffic coming from paid ads on other websites
* Email – Traffic arriving from your email subscribers

The best ways to increase organic search traffic are based on a huge list of Google ranking factors:

* Publishing content – Satisfying the needs of users by publishing content that contains keywords which they are searching for.

* Relevant keywords – Including relevant keywords (search terms) in your page title will encourage users to click on it and visit your website.
* Backlinks – Links from other relevant sites will significantly improve the organic rankings of a site.
* Usable site – Website usability, including parameters such as the time of loading and having no technical SEO errors, is crucial as a direct and indirect SEO factor.

When you rank well due to your organic results, usually, it is long-lasting. When you invest money in organic positioning then the results are more lasting, while money for paid search traffic is spent over and over again.

One of the most crucial factors in deciding whether to invest in efforts to increase your organic ranking and positioning is how the price of paid search traffic is determined.

The paid search ads price is determined based on your organic ranking: The more relevant your site is, the less the ads will cost.

Because the price of paid search traffic will reduce when your organic positioning increases higher in search results, then one of the most important things is to have as much organic traffic to your site as possible.

SEARCH ENGINE ALGORITHMS

Search engines are query machines that exist to organize the Internet's content and to offer the most relevant results to the questions that searchers are asking.

For your website to show up in search results, your content needs to be visible to search engines. That is the most basic rule of **Search Engine Optimization (SEO)**: if your site can't be found, there is no way you will show up in the search engine results page.

For determining the relevance of a website, search engines use algorithms which retrieve and sort stored information in a meaningful way.

How Search Engines Work

Search engines operate with three functions:

1. **Crawl** – Search the Internet for content, looking through the code and content of each URL they come across.
2. **Index** – Storing and organizing content found during the first step of crawling.
3. **Rank** – Providing pieces of content that will answer search queries in the best possible way, ranking results by relevancy.

Search Engine Crawling

Crawling is a process in which search engines dispatch a team of robots (usually referred to as crawlers or spiders) to find content, which can be an image, video, PDF, word document, or webpage. No matter the format, all content is discovered by links.

Making sure your site gets properly crawled and indexed is a prerequisite to showing up in the search engine results page.

Search Engine Index

Search engines store all information that they find in a vast database of all discovered content, which they deem suitable to show to searchers, called the search engine index.

Search Engine Ranking

When a search is performed, search engines retrieve content from their index of relevant content and then serve it in order of relevancy, which they deem will solve the searcher's query. Creating order in search results by relevance is known as ranking. If the search engine believes the website is more relevant to the search query, it will be ranked higher.

Based on the above, if your page is not showing anywhere in the search results or it is buried many pages back, the reasons are usually:

* Your website is new and therefore not yet crawled.
* Your website is not linked to from any external websites.

* Your site navigation makes it hard for a robot to crawl it properly.
* Your site contains some code that is blocking search engines.
* Your site has been penalized by a search engine for spam or shady tactics.

It is crucial to check with your website developer that crawlers avoid unimportant content by using proper tactics. And that the website is optimized in such a way that it will help search engines to find your relevant pages.

Common navigation mistakes that keep parts of your website hidden from crawlers are:

* Your desktop navigation shows different results than your mobile navigation.
* JavaScript enabled navigation can cause parts of sites to be hidden, so it's better to use HTML.
* Any type of personalization that serves different experiences to groups of customers.
* Not linking a primary page on your site to your navigation.

Therefore, your website must have clear navigation and helpful URL folder structures.

When search engines first emerged, it was much easier to use tricks and tactics, which were usually against guidelines, to rank higher on the search engine results page.

Such tactics don't work anymore, as search engines became more advanced and can now block non-relevant content by understanding the language behind it.

Essential Factors for High Ranking

Simply creating relevant content that search engines can easily crawl and index doesn't mean you will automatically rank well on the search engine results page.

To rank better than competitor sites that are of the same quality as yours, you need to create **authority**. That can be accomplished by getting links from high authority sites and building your brand while creating an audience that will engage with and amplify your content.

Search engines (such as Google) have confirmed that quality content and links are two of the three most important ranking factors for SEO.

Therefore, one of the significant steps in SEO and ranking well is to get links from other trustworthy sites.

Links can be one of two types:

*   Backlinks – Are external links from other websites pointing to your site.
*   Internal Links – Are links on your site that point to your other pages on the same site.

Backlinks are HTML hyperlinks that point from one website to another, and they act as real-life reputation. For example, if you ask four random people (which don't know each other) who is the best retailer in town, and they all say "DWR Retail" then you would be quite confident that "DWR Retail" is the best retailer in the city. That is precisely what backlinks do for a search engine; they confirm the reputation of a site.

Search engines treat backlinks as votes for importance and validity on the Internet.

If the site is popular and important, for example, like Wikipedia, then it can give importance to a website that it links to. Also, Wikipedia has millions of different sites linking to it, which proves its authority.

More backlinks leading to your site from other higher authority sites will cause your site to rank higher versus websites on the same subject.

Link Building

Backlinks can be editorially placed or earned.

Editorial links are the links added by sites and pages that want to link to your site.

A fundamental principle of collecting earned links is always through creating content that people wish to use, reference, and share. If you can provide exciting resources on the Internet, then people will have the desire to link to it. Creating content and bringing attention to it is all that you are required to do to get earned links.

Links from similar topic sites are generally higher valued than links from sites not relevant to your topic. For example, if your website sells mobile phones, then a link from a site on the topic of mobile phones will be much more valued than one about cat food.

Link building should never be only about search engine rankings. Instead, link building should be to bring qualified traffic to your website so that visitors will find value in your site.

The right partners of your company, or customers who like your brand, could give you backlinks by writing reviews of the product or you doing the same, then displaying it on their websites along with links back to your site.

Google recommends building a blog for your business as a valuable resource for backlinks generation, due to the unique ability to regularly push new material, consistently engage users, and generate conversations, all with the result of earning listings and links from other sites and blogs.

A local business that can reach the local community can result in excellent and influential links. Reaching the community can be in the form of:
* Sponsorships and scholarships
* Donations to needed causes
* Offering internships
* Organizing a local competition
* Promoting loyalty programs
* Organizing community events

Once you have content created for one social media channel from one event, you can simply slightly reformat it and use it for other social media and other channels.

Giving useful, interesting news about your company or product to bloggers, influencers, or press is a very effective method for link building. That can be achieved by simply giving a free, low-cost product to an Instagram or YouTube influencer that will create videos and do posts about your brand in return.

All the methods that are used to build links will also build your brand. Building backlinks is a great tool to promote your brand and products or services you offer.

Establishing authority through customer reviews can be crucial for your brand, as long as they are made by doing great things that make customers happy. Reviews are great content about your business that can be shared, which will ultimately earn you links from reputable sources.

Social Media Algorithms

Social media algorithms represent a complex way to do simple things. Complex in the sense that they are comprised of several hundred, if not thousand, lines of code, all working to do something straightforward. Their function is to provide social media users with content that is personalized and most relevant to them.

Facebook, Google, and virtually anyone running social media sites, know that users will only come back if they see what they like every time they log on. Algorithms are there to make that happen; they help ensure social media users aren't faced with content that is irrelevant to them.

By creating and publishing your content in a way that convinces social media algorithms that your content is relevant, then that algorithm will show and promote your content to the relevant audience. Sadly, this works both ways; if your content performs poorly in an algorithm relevance index, then it will be pushed to the back of the queue.

Despite their complexity, getting to grips with how social media algorithms work and developing ways to master them is not rocket science. In fact, most social media sites have clearly defined blueprints on how their algorithms handle "signals" to dictate what gets shown and to whom it gets shown at any point.

From this and through experience, it is easy to map out a strategy that exploits these algorithms in your favor.

User Interaction Is a Huge Flag No Algorithm Will Miss
When your content gets people talking, you are promoting what social media sites want in the first place, which is interaction and

user engagement. For that, you will be handsomely rewarded by their algorithms. It is important to note that algorithms track user interaction by measuring metrics like comments, likes, and shares.

Proven methods of pulling these metrics to your page are to create content that:

* Stimulates the interest of users
* Contains a call to action
* Speaks on a subject that users are passionate about
* Tags the people who matter

Social media hosts a deeply interconnected web of users. User A is connected to user B, and user B is connected to user C. Even though user C doesn't have a direct connection to user A, it's easy to see that a pathway for information spread – through user B – exists between user A and C.

The key takeaway here is that you do not necessarily need to be connected to everyone to reach everyone. Just one (or two, three) seeds is all it takes to make your social media forest flourish. So next time you create a post, make sure to tag influential users who relate with the content you are sharing. When you do that, you are shining a beacon for them (and everyone else linked to them) to see and interact with your content.

Timing Matters

There is such a thing as **peak hours** – the time when your audience base is most active on social media and **slow hours** – the period when they are mostly offline. Recognizing what time of the day these two periods fall under is the first step to making social media algorithms work for you.

That is because most social media algorithms are optimized to place a premium on time relevancy. They will want to show users more current information ahead of old posts. If most of your posts fall into the period when your users are offline, then they are more likely to land in the trash can of old posts. Avoid that by creating a social media timetable that takes peak hours into account.

The Bottom Line

Algorithms are there to pick out quality content from irrelevant content. Although one or two "black hat" methods to game the system might pop up once in a while, they are always short-lived. Worse still, they could get your content blacklisted. So, if you want to stay on top of algorithms, make sure to produce quality content consistently.

Consistency is critical for social media algorithms. For your audience to recognize your brand, you must be consistent. Being consistent in your social media brand allows you to grow in audience engagement and reach, satisfying both users and algorithms.

Social shares are not the same as backlinks, but shares to the correct people result in a backlink. Social shares increase traffic, visitors to your websites, increase brand awareness, and that results in the growth of trust and links. The connection between social signals and rankings is an indirect, yet essential part of the strategy.

Chapter 4

STRUCTURING CONTENT CREATION

Instead of using technology to automate processes, think about using technology to enhance human interaction.

Tony Zambito

RESOURCES IN CONTENT CREATION

RESOURCES FOR CONTENT CREATION ARE your team and tools. At the beginning of your content efforts, it is crucial to start simple with all the processes of creating content and doing online marketing more organically. That means not including too many people in the content creation or getting too many specialized tools to use in the content creation process.

TEAM

In the beginning, it is enough to start with one person that will work on creating and publishing content.

Later as you set the first steps in motion, you can bring in more people from different departments to participate or eventually even assign more people to the content team. Ultimately your goal should be that you have many employees from various departments gladly and willingly participating in content creation with ideas and content itself.

In any company, it is always possible to find a person that likes to create content instead of just being assigned to such a task.

Team responsibilities are content management and strategy, writing, editing, designing, publishing, and promoting.

One person can begin working alone, but once your marketing process evolves, then one person should never take care of more than three responsibilities at all times.

Always keep in mind that high-quality work is the primary goal of your team.

TOOLS

For productivity and consistency reasons, tools used in content creation are simple versions of:

* a content calendar
* social media calendar software
* graphic editor software
* WordPress templates
* analytics software
* data sharing

We'll take a look at each of these tools in turn.

Content Calendar

A content calendar is a shareable resource that teams use to plan all content activity, including social media. For example, publishing posts on blogs, forums, and all other available resources to a company.

A content calendar can be a simple excel file in a calendar-based format that will plan content as a rough sketch for a minimum of four months in advance. It's best is to open that file to everyone in the company so they can contribute with ideas.

For example, each Monday of the week could be a day for content about healthy living concerning your products or services, then Wednesday could be a day for celebrating your community, and so on.

Here *www.dariosipos.com/resources* you can download a free content calendar template.

Social Media Calendar Software

Consistency is crucial when publishing content on Social Media Networks. Therefore, it is necessary to publish posts at regular, popular times for each network. It's important that posting does not suffer because a team member is not available due to working on other company tasks.

Social media calendar software will enable you to maximize and streamline your social media processes. In the purest form, the software will do posting on all of your social media by a schedule that you put in place.

After you connect your social media profiles to software, set up a posting schedule for each social media profile separately, you can fill software with posts for months or years in advance. In short, when you use such software, you can focus your social media efforts on being quality instead of continually struggling to publish content at the correct time.

After publishing content not only will it show you analytics on how well you did but it will also store content in the archive, so, with a click of a button, you can re-publish it when needed.

All members of your team can log into the software and see what is scheduled for publishing, and make adjustments if necessary.

Such software comes with a pretty low price while enabling the right amount of automatization, and some of the most commonly used Social Media Calendars in the world are Buffer (*www.buffer.com*) and Hootsuite (*www.hootsuite.com*).

Graphics Editor Software

Graphic designers can create beautifully designed graphical material in different formats, but are expensive so are not needed in this content creation process. That alone will save you a lot of money and time in your content creation process.

The material itself is not needed in high resolution, as it usually would be for printing, which eliminates the need for high quality purchased stock photos.

What is needed is a tool that can perform simple reformatting of posts for different social media networks, and that can create many posts of similar nature with different free stock photos and text.

Such tools are: Canva (*www.canva.com*) with free and low-cost paid plans or the previously mentioned Buffer has a completely free tool named Pablo (*pablo.buffer.com*), including 600,000+ stock photos for free.

When it comes to creating professional videos at a low cost, you can use tools such as Promo (*www.promo.com*), which offers customization of their massive database of professionally done videos, together with complex editing made simple in a straightforward interface.

All mentioned tools are designed so they can be used by beginners without any specialized knowledge.

WordPress Templates

Creating a website for your brand or creating a blog would usually require you to hire a web developer that will also incur a substantial financial and time cost. Because, for months, you will be communicating on design and development back and forth. Most of the websites today on the Internet, including many successful webshops, are designed in WordPress because it enables users to change and add content easily.

Almost all web developers buy premade templates from specialized sites at a low cost, ranging from $20–$59. For example, one of the world's most popular WordPress themes for creating a news site is called Newspaper and comes at the cost of $59. Included in that price are fifteen different templates that will load a full news site with one click. In just a few hours, without technical knowledge, you can be operating your beautiful news site on top technology.

The largest depository of WordPress sites currently is ThemeForest (*www.themeforest.net*).

When you need to create a blog, brand page, or any type of page, first visit ThemeForest and compare price with the quote you got from a web developer. No matter what type of site you wish to create, it's highly likely that it already exists, pre-made, easy to install and at a low cost.

Analytics Software

To see how your online marketing efforts are progressing and how you compare to competitors, there are a few good software solutions.

When it comes to world rankings and country rankings, the world standard is the "Alexa Rank." The Alexa Rank parameter comes from a tool that can be seen on *www.alexa.com*, which is one of the most intuitive tools available for online analysis.

Alexa's suite of intuitive analytics will show you data in a way that you will quickly comprehend and be able to apply to the improvement of your company. From world ranks, country ranks, keywords gaps, organic and paid traffic share, to SEO errors, Alexa will teach you how to spot your opportunities quickly.

Probably the most useful tool is the "keyword gap matrix," which will display how your company compares to competitor keyword rankings. Or more simply, which competitor will be on top of search results after the user enters a search query common to you and your competitors.

SEMrush is another analytics tool that will help you discover your real competitors online, improve your SEO, and show you how to boost your rankings. SEMrush is advertised as an "all-inclusive suite for your marketing workflow" which is exactly what it does.

At the beginning of your content creation journey, it's recommended that you start with Alexa before moving to SEMrush.

There are other tools like SimilarWeb, Moz, and numerous others which could be suitable for your purpose.

Data Sharing

Content creation success is all about (or relies heavily on) your company empowering the workforce to make and share content ideas; there must be a smooth internal process that allows anyone in the business to contribute ideas.

From early on, the more sharing of data you manage to encourage, the easier it will be to create content ideas, and make all parts of the company contribute to your marketing success. That is especially important if you have multiple locations, for example, retail sales points, and there is a need to generate content from each store.

Ideally a platform for collaboration would be put in place, some of the popular solutions are Slack or Microsoft Teams.

Such a collaboration tool will keep all content in one place, and contribute to communication while motivating everyone to generate more of their own original content.

The Importance of Structure in Content Creation

Content marketing is an ongoing project, which can be laborious and time consuming. The tracking of all your efforts and planning future content can be overwhelming.

To keep your team aligned to company goals while ensuring everyone does their part, you need to set up a good structure.

The structure of creating your content marketing needs to be well organized and flexible, no matter if you are a small retailer or a big one. Only a good structure will enable you to endlessly create good content while keeping your team motivated.

If you are a small retail business and your team will grow later, then it's best to set up your content creation structure in such a way that it can easily be increased in size as you grow and evolve the process.

The organization is the main consideration in setting up a structure for your efforts. Ideally, all major tasks of your long-term plan should be broken into smaller pieces.

In content marketing, problems occur due to a lack of resources, or more often a lack of focus and structure. Some of the usual difficulties in content marketing are:

* Lack of expertise that can turn basic posts into great pieces of content
* Social media strategy that needs more precise tuning
* Process inefficiencies that consume time
* Improper set-up or lack of analytics

A great content marketing machine is made of many parts that are basically dependent on your team members, or better to say their roles. One of the major issues of even creating your content team arises from the way that companies hire employees and assign them roles. When companies need a person to run social media, they will publish a job advertisement for a social media manager. Despite seeming logical, it is not the best approach because it does not look at your content machine as a sum of all the parts.

Content marketing is complicated because it requires attention to detail: a detail that could completely change a piece. A person with a natural inclination for social media marketing will be able, with just a slight change of detail, to transform a basic post into a strong piece of content. Simply hiring a social media manager and telling them to manage social media channels will not be enough for success. Instead, you will have to figure out how that person fits into your content marketing machine and experiment with flexible roles. Job titles and roles constrict people and destroy their creativity: You need to allow and encourage full creative collaboration and experimentation.

There are people in your company who don't work in marketing but might have great ideas that will be valuable to your content marketing team. So, make sure the structure you build for content creation in your company empowers everyone to cooperate and to express their ideas freely, while not being constrained by their official job roles and titles.

The needs and desires of consumers change over time also. Therefore, you need to be flexible in content creation and be ready to make changes in any long-term plans.

STRUCTURING CONTENT CREATION

Now you know why it is so important to structure your content creation process, these are the steps to follow:

1. Fundamental ideas for content
2. Setting timelines
3. Creating content process
4. Reviewing content
5. Publishing content
6. Promoting content
7. Archiving content
8. Measuring results
9. Evolving process

Fundamental Ideas for Content
Everyone has ideas but they rarely turn into actual engaging content. Coming up with ideas for some period in advance can be challenging. If you lack original ideas, you can effortlessly search for them online.

Good ideas for content are answering some frequently asked questions from your customers, creating a free guide for your customers, or giving objective pieces of advice online about products or services.

Using Google Trends will reveal to you the subjects that people are searching for, so you can answer them in advance.

Asking colleagues in the customer service department for the most commonly asked questions will enable you to create a free online guide for service issues that customers will appreciate. Whatever type of content you create, you need to always keep in mind:

1. The buyer persona
2. The buyer journey

Buyer personas are built from the real words of real buyers, based on qualitative and quantitative research, telling you what potential customers are thinking as they study the product that you are offering to them. Buyer personas show you insights about your buyers' decisions.

The **buyer journey** is a set of factors that impact your potential buyers as they evaluate their options and select them.

A buyer journey has three stages:

1. **Awareness stage** – The prospect identifies there is a problem that needs a solution. Then the prospect researches possible solutions.
2. **Consideration stage** – The prospect has, after research, found a few potential solutions to their problem, after which they try to zero in on the best solution for their problem.
3. **Decision stage** – The prospect is ready to make a decision, which usually comes down to buying a product or service.

Content creation should always work for both the buyer persona and the buyer journey, otherwise you are wasting your time.

Setting Timelines

Keeping consistency is one of the crucial parts of your content strategy. Consistency is one of the factors which search engines are checking to determine if you are relevant in the field in which you publish content.

When you have established your fundamental content ideas, it's time to plan a timeline for the next quarter. This length of time is good as it covers a reasonable period but not too much, so you will be able to change content if necessary for any objective reasons.

At this stage, you should know all the company projects from all the departments (deals with suppliers, partnerships, events, trade fairs) and include them in your content timeline.

Creating Content Process

The process should name what each member of your team does, including any outside contractors (graphical designer or copywriter).

This simple outline of the content creation process is a great starting point:

*   General sketch of content
*   Draft of material
*   Editing
*   Design/Formatting

Reviewing Content

When content is created, you need an examination process that checks that the content matches the company branding, goals, SEO guidelines, and that it tells a story.

Usually, this step will create delay, so it's necessary to develop the process in such a way as to remove any delays by setting a timeline. Content guidelines should contain the roles of your team, deadlines, and how to check content against quality standards.

Tracking the progress of creation and editing can easily be done on teamworking software like Slack, Trello, or even Google Keep.

Publishing Content

After all previous steps are completed, the next step is publishing content.

Content can be published on social media, your webshop, brand website, blog pages, and others.

It's worth repeating: publishing content consistently is one of the crucial factors for success.

The best posting times and days for major social media networks you can download from: *www.dariosipos.com/resources*.

Social media calendars are the best method of keeping your team on track; schedule content in advance and make it visible to every member of the team for review and transparency.

Promoting Content

There are different channels where content can be promoted, ranging from social media, news sites, search engines, email campaigns, and many others. Each such channel has its own rules for a successful promotion.

Staying flexible in your content strategy is necessary to keep up with consumer society. Getting real people behind your content is also a crucial step to creating a community.

Archiving Content

Archiving your content is crucial as it can be used in the future with or without minimal modification. If you are a retailer, then there are regular times of year that usually have some similar type of promotions. Black Friday and other comparable sales always happen at the same time of the year, meaning that archived content can be reused.

Measuring Results

Measuring results is the conclusion of all of your steps, to determine what you did correctly and what needs to be improved.

The main result should be that you convinced more of the public to become your customers, which we will examine in detail later in this book.

Evolving Process

Your content strategy and content creation should always become better and better.

Your content strategy needs to keep up with your company development, market development, and new online trends.

Chapter 5

STORY BRANDING

Those who tell the stories rule the world.
Hopi American Indian proverb

SUCCESS THROUGH STORY BRANDING

A BRAND STORY IS A NARRATIVE that follows the facts and feelings that are created by your brand, products, or services. Unlike traditional advertising, which involves showing and telling people about your brand, a story must inspire an emotional reaction.

A big part of successful content creation in online marketing is to be able to create stories and build the brand through stories. Starting from your main company brand and spreading to each product or service that you offer.

The worst principle that can be applied online is to, through marketing efforts, convince customers that your company is the biggest hero among all your competitors. Such methods will have no results online and will push people away from your content and eventually prevent them from becoming your customer.

When Do Businesses Win Online?
Businesses win when they put the customer's story in front of their own stories.

Rarely companies have a problem with explaining the use of the products to users, as most products are not so innovative. At the same time, many companies do have a problem with how they speak about the products.

When a business hires a marketing agency, they often do not understand that firstly product messages need to be simplified into a great story. But, instead of simplifying messages, agencies tend to create more complex stories to justify their existence and fees.

Stories give form to complex situations and products. Stories get people and future customers interested and involved.

In the real world, words sell things much more than the web pages on which they are displayed.

Without simplifying and making your message and story clear, marketing is a waste of money, and not even the best product can beat a competitor that merely communicates better.

The Goal of Online Branding
The only goal of branding is that customers know where the brand is taking them.

That is because all humans have a simple goal in life; they all desire to be taken somewhere. To a better life, to a brighter future, or to participate in some movement bigger than just one person.

So, if you define how prospects' lives and experiences will be better if they do business with you, they will want to do business with you.

Speaking about customer problems will increase connection with your brand, which works much better than running slogans about how your company is the most impressive frog in the pond.

Businesses fail when marketing communications are not made on a regular human level. Human beings are always searching for ways to improve their lives and to find ways that will help them survive. So, create such a story that benefits your users, instead of speaking about your company story.

In crafting product messages, a sure win is to focus on the part of human psychology that causes people to search for ways to live better, survive, and feel better (primal needs, or Maslow's hierarchy of needs). Speaking about your own business does not help the customer with their primal needs. No one listens to speeches "about us".

Why Stories?

Creating stories is the most powerful tool in organizing complex information into something useful for customers, so that they will want to hear it.

People will always gladly walk into a story that helps them to achieve more in life or be more. The story should be simple and clear.

Noise in marketing is the real enemy of business, as it shuts down ideas and products more than anything else in the market. Readers will become customers based on what they hear and not what you say to them.

To get a sense of reality and check if customers understand you, do a simple test: ask your team members to describe your company product or brand message clearly and straightforwardly. If members of your own team are not able to summarize the company brand message clearly, then it is not likely they will be able to explain it to current and potential customers.

Start by creating a brand story from top to bottom: start with defining a brand story for your company, then departments, then move to your products.

Questions Guide a Story

A good story can hold our focus for hours, and a story is the best way to fight through the information noise that most humans are bombarded with every second of their life. The typical error is that brands speak about themselves and then randomly insert characters in their messages.

People buy products which they understand, more often than they buy the best products.

To make a company or product story simple and clear, use the following questions when crafting it:

1. What do customers desire?
2. What do customers not desire, or what blocks them from their desires?
3. How lost will the customer feel if they do not get their desires?

If those three questions are not answered in the product message, then the customer gets lost in too many similar words.

Any part of the story that doesn't explain these three fundamental issues needs to be removed. All elements which do not serve the story, need to go.

Then just formulate the story even better by using this pattern of questions:

1. What do you offer?
2. How does your offer make customers' lives better?
3. How do customers get or purchases what you offer?

Sometimes, it might seem that this is an impossible task, for example if the company provides more than one service or sells complex products. Even in those case the message still needs to be simple enough to sell the product. There is one umbrella message summarizing all that you do; it just requires creativity to find it.

The Main Character of a Story

The customer is the only main character in the story that you tell the customer about yourself or your product.

Brand or Product is never the main character of a story. Product suppliers are only a guide for a customer, who is on a journey to become a superstar – with the supplier's help.

The most powerful presentations are made when the customer is positioned as the main character, and the business as a guide who provides wisdom, products, or services that enable the customer to progress in his life.

Once you identify what customers want, then you will know which story will attract their attention.

What Customers Solve with Purchases

Brands and companies need to focus on three levels of a problem (frustration) that exist for customers: internal, external, and philosophical.

An example is that the customer wakes up one day, and his coffee machine stops working (external problem), which makes the customer feel insecure during the day due to sleepiness (internal problem). Then there is a philosophical dilemma: "If only there was a coffee machine that could solve more essential issues in the world than just preparing coffee."

Philosophical problems are defined as a more substantial, more in-depth story for a customer that our brand is on a mission to solve. For example, good must prevail over evil.

Customers are searching for a solution for their internal problems, which would help them to become successful in life and solve problems that are disrupting their experience of life. Most companies are selling solutions for external problems and do not realize that customers never buy products to solve only those problems. So, those companies are not living and understanding their full story.

Framing your solutions to address internal, external, and possibly philosophical problems immediately increases the value of your brand in the customer's eyes.

CREATING A GREAT STORY

The main character of a story is your future customer who always searches for ways that can help them to achieve what they want in life.

The leading cause of frustration to a customer is the one single enemy causing it, even if there are many contributing factors. So, it's best to define the single enemy and make it relatable and real.

To create a movie or book, like a brand story, you need to make a space between the main character and their goals. If you are not able to define what the customer wants, you cannot create the plot and a happy ending.

Customers need to understand what is their enemy in the story, and that the offered product will help them win over that enemy.

Customers are looking for a guide in life who will help them, not another main character of their story. So, companies that position themselves as the main character in customers' stories will actually compete with customers. People should always be the main character of their own stories.

Humans focus on primitive survival instincts: food, warmth, happiness, having children. So, we can relate that to the modern way of life as having money, building social networks, buying luxury items.

Luxury item purchases belong to one of the primal human instincts: being associated with power, which can help humans to survive.

The desire for meaning is one of the most influential motivators, as life becomes intolerable without a purpose. Therefore, craft a message that will invite the customer to participate in something bigger than just one single purchase.

Customers only trust a business that has a clear plan, which eliminates any confusion on how to do business with them; that plan needs to be an essential part of the story.

Being a Good Guide

Everyone is looking for a guide in life, and when companies position themselves as something else than a guide, they are destined to fail.

In real stories, as in movies or books, the main characters are usually weak, so when companies position themselves as strong with a desire to be the hero, that is the sure path to self-destruction.

How does a company be a good guide? The guides have authority and empathy. Customers trust companies that understand them.

How to express authority without bragging in marketing materials:

1. Customer testimonials
2. Stats on the number of customers
3. Rewards which you received
4. Existing customer logos

The first question customers will have when speaking with you or looking at your marketing materials is: "Can I trust this brand, and can I respect this brand?"

Stepping Stones to a Purchase

Customers trust a Guide that gives them a plan.

Purchasing is a sign of a serious relationship and not a causal one, so you need to provide a plan.

Customers can lose something when they do business with you, and that makes them skeptical and nervous. So, create a route (a plan) for a customer that will guide them in purchasing from you, and solve all the issues which the customer might have in their head. Any confusion in a plan which guides the customer to the solution of their problems will make them quit the purchase process.

Usually, there should not be more than four or five steps when guiding the customer through purchase, and if you deal with selling complex products or services, then you can split numerous steps into phases so that it will be streamlined to a few steps.

Making agreements with the customer, such as a customer satisfaction agreement, will increase trust in a product because the customer has a plan that makes it clear how to do business with you without risk.

Offering the customer a hassle-free returns policy is a perfect example of increasing trust in a product, brand, and your company as a supplier.

Tell Them to Buy
Customers will move to purchase only when they are called to action, and the story which is provided needs to force them to take action.

Never assume that customers understand how the product improves their life, and a good way to make sure they know is to mention it to them endlessly.

That call to action will enable them to live better and avoid a tragic ending, so be confident in asking them to make a good thing for themselves.

Two calls to action are efficient: A **direct call to action** and a **transitional call to action**, which creates a future long-term relationship.

When you create a guide for a customer that will take them through the process of purchasing, and you solve their internal, external, and philosophical problems, then complete the last part of the story and call them to action or, in other words, to commit to a purchase. People never make significant life decisions without the external pressure of a call to action, instead choosing to remain in their comfort zone.

For a company that sells products, it is apparent that a seller wants the customer to make a purchase, but that does not mean it is also evident to the customer. Always invite people to make a purchase that will improve their lives.

Direct calls to action are: order now, call today, register today.

Transitional calls to action are based on the principle of giving the customer something of value, and they will return for more: free guides, free samples, and free advice.

People are drawn to simple solutions, so do your best to offer simple solutions as it will positively separate you from the competitors.

Fear Appeal Spice

Loss, can be a significant motivator for customers in the decision--making process.

Brands that don't warn customers what they will lose without getting their product will never be successful. Including bullet points outlining what the customer will lose without your product is merely best practice behavioral science in a commercial offer.

Give to customers, after explaining to them what the threat is, an action plan that protects them against a danger and challenges them to take that specific action.

Too much fear appeal to the story could block a customer from doing anything. However, merely explain to customers what negative things in life they will have by not using your product.

DESIGN OF A GOOD STORY

Never assume that people know how you can change their lives and always keep telling them.

Tell customers how their lives will look like if they buy your product. There are three good endings to each customer story:

1. **Achieving power and position** – Create exclusivity by membership, identity association.
2. **A union that makes the hero complete** – Reduced anxiety, more personal time, reduced workload.
3. **Acceptance** – Need to reach potential, inspiration, acceptance as they are, transcendence.

To make people follow us, we need to tell them where we are taking them. Pictures of happy smiling customers are the perfect ending to any story.

People Want Brands to Help Them Change
The most significant factor that motivates customers to purchase your product is being better than they currently are. Moreover, the human desire to transform is a big motivator.

Smart brands will show their customers an appealing, new identity, which they aspire to, and then offer a guide on how to acquire that new and appealing identity.

As a brand, leading customers to change is more than marketing: itis an act bigger than life. The best brands are dedicated to the transformation of the customer into a better version of themselves.

All people dream of being taken somewhere further, that is a true branding secret.

Chapter 6.

DEVELOPING CONTENT IDEAS

Without strategy, content is just stuff, and the world has enough stuff.

Arjun Basu

PROCESS FOR GENERATING CONTENT IDEAS

GENERATING NEW IDEAS IS A daily part of life when working in marketing, but with the need to create specific designs for a particular purpose the task suddenly becomes harder.

As your business depends on the content, you have to generate content ideas without a break and keep idea generation smooth. For that reason, it is essential to have a well-defined process.

As the people in charge of content most likely have other tasks to keep them busy, it is essential to structure the content creation process. Because in stressful periods, which demand more content creation (during any sale period, for example), only a well-established process will ensure that content is consistently created and published.

The main purpose of the content creation process is to create a predictable stream of original, quality, and relevant content.

Having other members of the team actively help you to create content will be of the highest value because other people's contributions will generate more of your ideas.

At the beginning of content creation there will be no lack of content ideas, but as you get forced to generate more of them with a specific purpose, the lack of ideas will settle in.

Having a process will enable the increasing pace and quantity of content created.

Inspiration for content is also the correct part of the process that you need to assign to your team. Getting inspired for new ideas requires that you build upon old already existing ideas of your own.

The process of getting content ideas comes down to collecting raw materials (from events or daily business), and brainstorming around them.

The Internet is an endless source of ideas, therefore start consuming all kinds of content ideas from a search engine, and don't stick only to your niche of retail. Add yourself to groups on LinkedIn, follow stories on Instagram, or use other channels to find ideas.

Make sure someone from your team regularly monitors competition and provides you information on any good idea that they are using for their content marketing.

CREATING CONTENT IDEAS

To create your content ideas, when you are just starting out, assign one person, and then later include your full team (from logistics, sales, and other departments). One person should be in charge of technical details and complete the overall process, then include other members of the team to help generate ideas.

That person should follow these steps for successful idea generation:

1. Research the buyer persona's favorite type of content.
2. Check what people discuss on social media, forums, online blogs, or any other online resources. There you can see what bothers existing customers and what they would love to read about, usually it's solutions to their most common problems. You can even make online queries to ask users what they like.
3. Determine what competitors and similar sites are doing. For example, if you sell consumer electronics, then your

audience probably likes gadgets. Locate a news site dedicated to gadgets; there you will find a bunch of ideas and already sharable content. From research tools such as Amazon's Alexa and SEMrush, you can check which competitor is doing exceptionally well and follow their feed for some ideas.

4. Find fresh, authoritative and relevant content to share from specialized news and article generator sites. One such site that works exceptionally well is Right Relevance (*www.rightrelevance.com*), which offers free account registration.

5. Research the organic keywords (See chapter 3) that the audience are most interested in so that you can write content following the rules of search engine optimization. The most common keywords that your target audience researched can be studied for free on Google Trends.

6. Inform all company departments that content ideas are welcome, this will definitely generate some exciting topics.

7. Regularly sit with any employee who could contribute, including the content team, and have dedicated sessions just to brainstorm ideas.

THE IMPORTANCE OF LONG-TERM CONTENT PLANNING

Ninety percent of effective retailers have a person driving their content strategy. Having a road map for content is essential.

The role of content is driving a customer through the process of attracting customers. Content is an integral part of each stage in the buyer journey.

It is necessary to remain active in regards to your competition, monitor what they do, and be able to change your strategy if competition comes up with something revolutionary.

Also, it is essential to be consistent with content each day, each week, and month after month. Only consistent effort will give you the option to grow your content base and find new channels and content opportunities.

Content creation is not support for the marketing team but for sales efforts, customers, product managers, and other sales processes in the company. The content team should be aligned with the overall goals of the organization.

Long-term planning will take customers through the buyer journey. Content keeps your marketing and sales efforts running. When content is relevant, then you will be able to answer all customer questions in advance.

Building a Long-term Content Strategy
A marketing funnel that is aligned with the buyer journey is the central principal of your marketing engine.

Inbound Marketing Methodology is a process that targets potential customers at different levels of product and brand awareness. It is all about getting found online, through search engines and on social media. It promotes earning a prospect's attention, as opposed to renting it by paying for ads.

The Buyer's Journey and Content

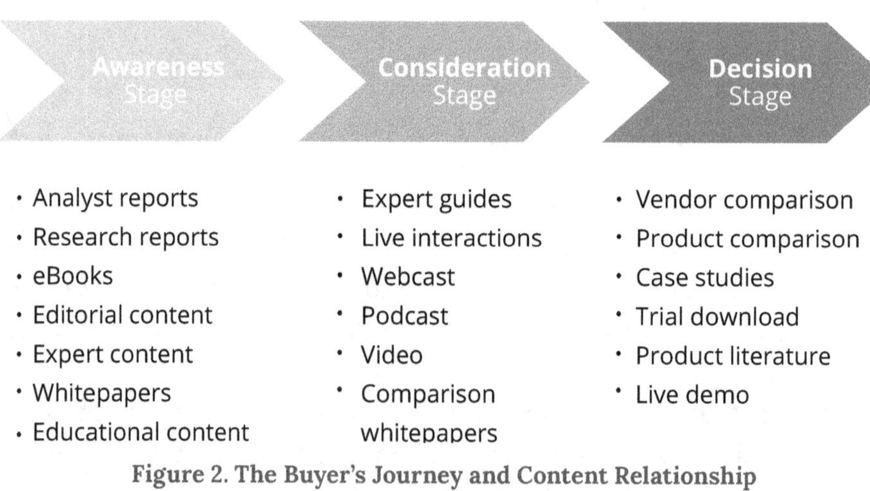

Figure 2. The Buyer's Journey and Content Relationship
Source: HubSpot

As visible in the above illustration, long-term planning is required to be able to create such quantity and scope of content and materials. At each stage, we can see that different types of content are more beneficial.

A **marketing engine** relates each stage of the buyer journey to a marketing funnel stage as follows:

* The awareness stage relates to visits and leads.
* The consideration stage relates to marketing qualified leads, or sales qualified leads.
* The decision stage relates to opportunities and customers.

Marketing engines require a long-term strategy to be successfully built.

To create a long-term strategy, first set your marketing goals, then check what assets your company has or needs then create your buyer journey for your buyer personas.

Setting marketing goals will enable you to connect your short-term efforts with a long-term strategy.

How to Inspire your Content Team to Have Great Ideas

As a manager or content marketer, one of the most challenging issues you will face as you navigate the tricky terrain of creating engaging content is churning out worthwhile content ideas, on a steady basis.

For most content curators, idea creation is a painstaking process, one that, over time, becomes ineffective and challenging to execute. The good news is that it doesn't have to be this way. Your content team and other members of your company can join in on this task to make it a more fluid and seamless process. Here's how to inspire them to do just that.

Start by Defining What's Holding Your Team Back

It's rare that members of a content creation team don't have ideas of their own. Most of the time, however, these ideas fail to reach the spotlight because there is a hindering factor playing out in the background. As a leader seeking to optimize your idea generation process, the first step is identifying this hindering factor.

Hindering factors could take on many forms, while from experience, the following typically appear in the workplace environment:

* Lack of confidence among team members

* Nonchalant attitude
* Micromanagement from the leader
* A culture of idea rejection

The trick to singling out the particular limiting factor is to establish a discussion round table, one where you step back and converse with your members as a peer, rather than a team leader. Once you have identified the problem, it is a simple case of taking steps to remedy it.

Create an Atmosphere of Freedom

If someone is doing the heavy lifting, why bother? We imagine that is the thought process of your team when you shoulder the entirety of the idea creation process. If that is the case, then it is about time you transfer the responsibility, or part of it, to team members. Give your team the room to come up with ideas on their own.

Doing this strengthens their ability to function independently, and where independence thrives so does creativity and innovation, all of which are key to deriving stellar content ideas.

Working as a Team

Two good heads are better than one, is a famous saying. While it is easy to assume that a content creation team will always function as a composite whole, in reality fragmentation and isolation are the paths most members will take. When you transfer the reigns of idea creation to the team, you will find that most team members will take on the approach of brainstorming individually to come up with ideas.

That method is, however, counterproductive. If brilliant ideas are to flourish, then your team must think as a collective. Ideas can be generated in a silo, but the task of determining which is a better fit, in terms of organization-specific goals and objectives, should be undertaken by the group and as a team.

Constructive Criticism

Criticism comes in various forms, and you've probably heard that constructive criticism is the way to go. That is because constructive criticism is a positive reinforcement mechanism that actively applauds positives while highlighting the negatives.

Note that the process of criticizing constructively involves highlighting what is wrong. Your team needs both sides of the picture; give praise when deserved, and reprimand where necessary. It is called criticism for a reason. One mistake many managers make is to de-emphasize the criticism. In practice, that only broods an irregular idea creation atmosphere. Your team needs to understand what is wrong with an idea, if there is anything wrong in it; just never make it the point of emphasis over and above the positives.

Idea Creation Is Best Undertaken as a Continuous Process
Unlike the start-stop process of creating content, designing an idea is an endeavor that must be orchestrated seamlessly if it is to work in the long term. That is a roundabout way of saying your team must integrate the process of deriving ideas into their daily workflow as opposed to scheduling specific periods for brainstorming.

The latter approach, over time, mounts undue pressure on the team. The former, better known as **rolling ideation**, allows your team to create ideas on the fly, without pressure and without the limitations that come with organized sessions. Rough ideas derived through the week can then be fine-tuned at scheduled team brainstorming sessions later on.

In sum, inspiring your team to join in on the idea creation process is all about creating a positive environment where creativity, freedom, and team spirit all thrive. As a team leader your job is to provide this enabling environment and then check the excesses by giving constructive criticism

Chapter 7

WRITING LIKE AN EFFICIENT WRITER

If your content isn't driving conversation, you're doing it wrong.

Dan Roth

EFFICIENT WRITING

COMPELLING CONTENT IS RELEVANT AND useful to your readers. Your writing should speak in the language of a customer, on a customer level, and discuss problems that they have.

To make users read your content, it has to be helpful and useful. Only then will people connect with you. When you show your expertise to customers, positioning yourself as a guide, then they will start to trust you. That relationship where you are guiding the reader to the solution of their problem will create great trust.

Traditional media communicates using "one-to-many" platforms, conversely online communication is "many-to-many." People's increased trust in peer-to-peer communication minimizes the influence of traditional advertising. A major sin today in marketing is a lack of relevance.

The new reality of marketing online is that the public creates marketing messages instead of marketing departments. In engaging customers online over the long term, it will not be clear where marketing stops and selling starts. In a connected world where people have numerous channels for communication, the most crucial channel is word-of-mouth.

We've covered how publishing relevant product content is key but it's just one of the necessary steps. Making that content available where people can find it is the next step. Develop a keyword strategy to target keywords that people enter in search engines. Seek "long-tail keywords" in the form of three words or longer phrases, and include them in your communications. Also, make sure your content is worthy of sharing. There is nothing more effective than people sharing your content on their social network sites.

Today, it doesn't matter what companies say about themselves; it is what others say about them that really matters.

The online and physical retail worlds now routinely merge. Location-based interactions allow companies to offer customers promotions and discounts while they shop. More than before, the retail reality is consolidating online and offline spheres.

Engaging with Efficient Content

When you analyze successful online content, you will notice a pattern in the types of content that are usually more popular than the average: They're created based on satisfying human psychology.

There are approximately twenty-one themes of content that all humans crave and they like to read and engage with online. Content that:

1. Reminds us life is short
2. Reminds us dreams can come true
3. Gives us faith to believe in bigger things
4. Reminds us that we matter
5. Reminds us of the overlooked or forgotten "basics"
6. Has unexpected twists
7. Tells us a story
8. Takes us along on a journey
9. Inspires us to action
10. Makes us laugh or smile
11. Makes us cry (tears of joy or sadness)
12. Reveals secrets
13. Surprises us

14. Encourages us never to give up
15. Reminds us that we are one-of-a-kind and encourages us to live that way
16. Reminds us that there is more
17. Confirms our assumptions
18. Challenges our assumptions
19. Educates us while entertaining us
20. Involves David defeating Goliath
21. Gives us a fresh point of view even about everyday things

Formulating your content based on the themes mentioned above will, for sure, create content that appeals to your readers. At *www.dariosipos.com/resources* you can download a helpful infographic with types of content that all humans crave.

Additionally, applying the below elements to your writing, will add to your content success:

* Using an attention-grabbing headline
* Writing in a tone relevant to readers
* Including content that helps the reader to understand a topic better
* Adding to the conversation instead of recycling content that exists
* Writing content in a way that people perform a search
* Building a structure (use subheadings)
* Choosing one central idea of writing
* Supporting your brand message, value, and strategy
* Inserting a call to action
* Checking for grammatical errors

When you write, cut out anything that does not support your main idea while writing in simple language using an active voice. Be clear and concise.

Write for a specific platform, making sure that your tone of voice and way of writing fit the platform for which you are writing. Use short sentences and paragraphs. Remove extra words or corporate jargon. Be conversational even more by using "you" and "your" in writing.

WRITING POWERFUL HEADLINES

A catchy headline is your opportunity to gain the browser and convert them to a reader. Based on some studies done by Nielsen Norman Group, around 80% of visitors, when reading longer posts, will read a headline but only 20% will actually finish reading it.

Headlines can be post headlines, headlines of articles, or headlines of product listings on your e-commerce site. Bad headlines will cause your content marketing to fail.

Steps to writing powerful headlines:

* Use specific numbers and data.
* Use underlying reason.
* Call for attention.
* Use headline formulas.

Usually, above sixty-two characters search engines ignore the remainder of the headline.

Use Specific Numbers and Data

Headlines create around 52% of the effectiveness of your posts. Research shows that headlines containing numbers can generate up to 70% more engagement. Odd numbers in the headline will have more success than even numbers in about twenty percent of cases.

When writing headlines, use numerals instead of words for numbers, because that too is a successful step to better engagement and a shorter, more straightforward headline.

If you are creating guides for customers for any field (after-sales service guide, for example), then never use more than nine steps.

Use Underlying Reason

In a headline, use the underlying reason why some action should be done, giving people a good reason to read your content.

The best words to include in your headlines are: Reasons, Lessons, Ideas, Tips, Tricks, Facts, Secrets, Strategies.

Some examples:

5 Reasons Why Having a New Phone is a Must

9 Facts About Your Phone That You Didn't know

3 Secrets to Buying a Cheap TV

Call for Attention

The headline should make the viewer read the first sentence and call for attention because attention spans are on average just eight seconds. There is no such thing as excellent content without a captivating headline that will grab the reader's attention.

The headline can convince your readers to continue reading your posts until the end.

Any successful headline should apply these four rules:
* Communicate that the subject is useful.
* Include urgency in it.
* Make it unique.
* Be very specific.

E-commerce sites use urgency and scarcity in high quantities. Amazon uses both elements on their product pages: urgency appears as "you save", and scarcity as "only X pieces left in stock."

Use Headline Formulas

As you create your content process, you will discover formulas for headlines that work for you. Usually, content is created before writing a headline because you will be able to match the headline much better with the text after it is written.

One of the formulas, for example, is to identify the problem, offer a solution, make a promise the solution will work.

A headline is an integral part of your content no matter the format, but when writing longer posts, the introduction, subtitles, bullet points, and call to action are equally important.

The best approach is to use storytelling (story branding) and data-driven content to build your authority, all while solving the reader's problems.

Catching Attention in Under Six Seconds

The attention span of humans is now on average shorter than ever before – about eight seconds.

Getting hold of people's attention is a dicey game of hit and miss; with the vast deluge of information permeating our cyberspace every single minute, it is hard to keep focus and focus on what is important.

If you're a content publisher looking to grab scarce attention, here are five strategies to consider:

* Make it simple, concise, and relatable
* Master content delivery channels
* Include video
* Take the direct approach
* Include interactive content

Simple, Concise, and Relatable

People hate what they find hard to understand. If you are going to catch them and keep them hooked, then whatever information you are presenting must be easy to understand and easy to relate with, especially in the first instance. An excellent way to do this is to introduce what you are trying to present by piggybacking it on a familiar concept.

As an example, if you are trying to introduce a new product into the market, you can hit the mark by outlining a problem with the competition's product that yours does away with. Your audience is already familiar with the competitor product, and you are offering something better. Sometimes, that is all the information they need to keep their faces glued to the screen.

Mastering Content Delivery Channels

Every digital platform – the media through which most content gets to end-users – has its own peculiar set of written and unwritten rules.

When you know these rules (and all the blind spots), it becomes easier to present your information in the manner that appeals best to your target demographic. The more audience-specific or tailored your content is, the more engaging it will turn out to be.

Of course, these rules vary across the board for different digital platforms. Twitter, for instance, is the revered home for short and spicy bursts of information, so naturally, you will want to keep it toned down on there. Audiences on LinkedIn – a site for professionals – will, on the other hand, prefer detailed expositions on any subject matter.

Including Video

If you have been a publisher for long enough, then you have probably come across the popular "video is everything" school of thought – every major digital platform is moving towards video, and you should too. Well, not quite. While video does remain a high-impact content distribution format, it is not a magic wand to fix all your engagement and conversion problems.

If you push bland unoptimized content through video, it will change very little. Worse still, it can actually hurt your current engagement. What you can do with video, however, is to present otherwise bland content in a captivating way. "Captivating" can be very subjective, but some evergreen strategies include, spicing it up with humor, artistry, controversy, or better still, all three.

Taking the Direct Approach

Sometimes all your audience needs to keep up with you is an answer to the question "why should I listen to you?" And sometimes, the perfect answer to this question is a simple truth. You have probably, at one point, come across fishy articles, videos, or ads with what we like to call "clickbait" titles. Something along the lines of:

"This man shares the secret to making millions from home."

"How to succeed in an office environment."

"This is exactly how algorithms work."

These titles will get clicks because they provide direct answers to questions many people have on their minds. You, too, can grab the attention of your audience by giving straightforward answers to the questions that are on their minds.

Interactive Content

The Internet is very one-dimensional. Everyone is pushing tons of content to internet users, and no one bothers about their side of the story. As an internet user myself, trust me when I say it can get exhaustive and not to mention boring.

Making content interactive will prevent it from being dull and exhaustive.

When content is presented as a two-way street, one where a publisher releases content and the input of the audience is sought and appreciated, then the user feels the need to interact with the publisher. So, when the users want to interact with you as a publisher then, congratulations, you have successfully captured their attention. The best part? It is not just for eight seconds – you get to decide how long you want to keep them hooked.

CREATING MEDIA PLATFORMS

Where the Internet is about availability of information, blogging is about making information creation available to anyone.

George Siemens

REASONS TO OWN A BLOG

RETAILERS CAN USE THEIR BLOGS to connect with people, get feedback, and provide personalized promotions for products.

If you manage your social media channel for years while investing a significant amount of work and money in promotion, primarily if you invest in paid advertisement, then your social media channels are quite valuable to your business.

Changes in the way social media channels display content, often caused by the corporate owners simply updating guidelines, can result in a loss of followers that you have built up over years. So, all your efforts and money will be gone. Such changes happen more often than you think.

A great way to prevent this is to own your resources. One of the ways to own your resources is to create your own blogs, channels, and platforms.

A blog is both a media type and a channel, and not merely a social media channel. A blog can be used to collect user's email addresses, which you then can use for future promotions without paying for ads, and content from a blog can be used as material for the social media channels.

When you operate a "neutral" blog, which is publishing independent reviews of similar products on the market, then you have a chance to influence readers more than when you run a blog on your webshop, promoting just your products.

People like to read neutral opinions on subjects, such as "3 Tips on How to Buy a Great Cheap TV" and "Top 5 Ways to Save Money When Shopping". People will trust a neutral source more than you saying your company is "the best retailer". On average, humans require three confirmations of a fact to believe it.

Many famous brands own such "blogs" which pretend to be neutral, while in reality they have an agenda behind them. They are not called "blogs" but pretend to be independent media carrying imaginative names.

When you own your blog, you should still place your content to all other possible blogs not owned by you. Whenever you publish a blog post, you are creating a new unique page online. That increases your chances to rank higher, and other links are going back to you if your site is published on your social media.

People interested in your content will also be interested in your offer and products, so your blog also could collect readers' email addresses in a non-intrusive way.

You can use your blog to strategically promote your offers and brand, by providing solutions to readers' problems.

A blog that you own will be able to publish and promote content regularly without the delays of third parties. It will help you to attract new visitors and convert them into potential customers.

Except for the word "blog," the only things that separates you from traditional media is the quantity of original content that you are able to produce.

CREATING YOUR BLOG

People tend by nature to listen to bits of advice on what to purchase from sites that are not connected with the seller. Also, people will always tend to listen to pieces of advice more from an independent "newspaper-like" webpage than just a blog post.

When it comes to blog types, there are three options for most retailers:

1. Operate a blog on your e-commerce page within the same URL domain.
2. Operate a blog on another external URL domain visibly associated with your business.
3. Operate your own newspaper-like site as an independent media platform to provide a neutral opinion to the readers.

The first option, to operate a blog on your e-commerce page within the same domain, is just a matter of asking your web developer to create an internal subpage, and then publish content to it.

The second option, to run your blog on another domain, can be very quickly further developed to be an independent media platform for your business under the third option.

The exact steps of starting a blog are:

1. Decide on the main subject of your blog (example: gadgets, home appliances, gaming, or other).
2. Register the appropriate domain that reflects the topic in the URL for the blog and hosting. Make sure to create a name connected with the subject and add in the headline some word indicating "newspaper" type of content (news, magazine, times, journal, digest).
3. Go to *www.themeforest.com* and locate a WordPress Theme named "Newspaper Theme X" by producer "tagDiv" with a cost of approximately $59.
4. Within a few clicks, by following the user manuals, install both WordPress and the Newspaper Theme then also install preloaded content with a single mouse click.
5. The result is that now you have a Newspaper page looking highly professional in line with top world media sites, already with preloaded content, so you can start publishing your own content right away.

When choosing a URL domain, you can keep ownership of the domain hidden, by merely paying a low extra fee, which is the standard behavior of all significant international brands. On your new blog, or better to say Newspaper, don't display your logos or connect the site with your business.

The idea here is to perform neutral comparing of products and brands, and then nudge users slightly with the conclusion that your brand is the best.

How do you do that while being truthful? Simply by choosing to speak about the benefits of your product or brand that are really better than competitors. Your brand or product always does have some advantage over competitors, or else it would not even exist. Focus on finding and writing definite advantages over the competition.

The mentioned "Newspaper Theme" has the highest number of sales in the world from all similar themes, and powers most of the professional newspapers and blogs that you see on the Internet. Managing WordPress and the Newspaper Theme requires a maximum of two days of learning effort, in case you are a complete beginner.

The optional step for later is to add your newspaper page to Google News, which means your content will show up in Google News Alerts. Detailed rules and procedures on how to do that are available on Google News itself.

Some examples of great blogs that are actually full-scale media platforms are: *www.digitalfuturetimes.com* and *www.retailnewsmagazine.com*

MANAGING A BLOG

When starting a retail business blog, you need to outline the responsibilities of everyone involved. Creating and maintaining a blog is a long-term commitment. When creating a blog, you need to create one that nurtures only simple objectives and avoids complexity.

No matter that you own the blog and your marketing team manages it, as soon as possible you should also invite outside authors to contribute. Planning before launching will make your blog successful.

The steps for running a blog are:

1. Invest the time necessary by experimenting and finding what users like to read.
2. Be involved and care for your topic.
3. If the blog does not work well, then change the main subject till you find one that works.
4. Stick at it long term, keep going because blogging is a long-term investment.

To keep the blog interesting, your plan should cover the following areas:

* Write openly about your company in the form of conversation; you need to be ready to have a conversation with people.
* Write dynamic blog posts instead of neutral, so your blog posts should be more compelling than your newsletters.
* Invite your co-workers from around the company to contribute, because they will know your culture.

Parameters by which you measure the effectiveness of your blog can be:

1. Unique visitors
2. Pageviews
3. Amount of time visitors remain on a page
4. The bounce rate of people on the page

Your content marketers should create a content plan that will contain blog goals, targeted readers, and core topics.

In the beginning, you can acquire part of the content by reposting other articles from other blogs. As long as you mention the Author and Source that is allowed, and the author will actually be happy that you are using his content and referring to him.

Pages where you can find relevant articles for your site are aggregators of articles, such as *www.rightrelevance.com.*

As your news site progresses with content, you can ask some authors to contribute directly with their article to your site. Additionally, it is quite usual that very soon, you will start getting enquiries to publish articles from authors that are trying to begin their writing career.

The best publishing schedule will see you reposting two or three posts from other sites, and then writing and publishing one unique post.

Please refer to chapters 2 – 7 for guidelines on how to create great content and story branding.

Great content is the foundation of your efforts. It attracts visitors to your site, increases trust, and builds relationships. Repurposing successful content to other media will be successful.

Once when your content is published, you should reshare it to all of your social media channels, and offer it to other social media channels and blogs. Most of the independent blogs are in desperate need of content daily. Therefore, any interesting material provided to them will most likely be used right away.

Warning Signs That You Are Creating Irrelevant Content

The phrase "content is king" was coined shortly after search engines came into existence. At that time, all that content publishers needed to do to be successful was to flood the Internet with as much content as they could create. Pushing out as much content as possible – like casting many nets at sea – was the sure-fire way to pull in the haul (read: internet traffic), or so they thought.

As it turns out, pushing out content in droves was not the secret to driving engagement. For that, you will need a healthy dose of informative, educative, and, more importantly, relevant content. To help guard your steps and help keep you within the confines of relevance, here are five warning signs that pop up when you are producing irrelevant content.

Your Content Is Not Picking Up Organic Steam

How much organic engagement do your publications attract on their own? If the number is towards the lower limit of the average traffic statistic for your niche, then you are most likely producing content that is inapplicable to your audience. In other words, it is irrelevant.

You must understand just what your audience wants. When you publish content that falls outside the scope of audience interest, it is less likely to convert into clicks regardless of how superb your content is. It makes no sense, for instance, to throw scientific articles at an audience that is begging for a daily dose of celebrity gossip.

It Fails Grossly at Answering Any Specific Questions

The Internet, and more especially search engines, are filled with users searching for answers to a myriad of questions. It is no surprise that the vast bulk of Google search queries revolve around "how-tos", "where-tos", and "what-tos". When you produce content with an intent to strike the bells of relevancy, it should ideally provide answers to the questions members of your target audience are most likely to pose.

You Have Visitors All Right,
But None of Them Stay for Long Enough

The amount of time visitors spend on your content, measurable with KPIs like bounce rates and time-on-page, paints a vivid picture of how relevant your content is to the viewing audience. If they spend very little time, indicated by a high bounce rate, then it means you have failed to grab their attention. If your content is not getting their attention, then it is, by all means, irrelevant to them.

Your Search Engine Ranking Is Tumbling

Search engine algorithms pay keen attention to vital signals that point them to what people like to see. If people shy away from your content (indicating that it is irrelevant to them), search engine algorithms take note. And the penalty for that is that your publications get relegated to the end of the list, far off from the top of search rankings.

So, next time you search for keywords you have blended into your content and your page fails to turn up in search engine listings reassess yourself, it could be that the material was irrelevant in the first place.

Your Keywords Don't Reflect Your Audiences' Habits

In drumming up a viable content strategy, it is easy to fall down the rabbit hole of creating keywords that sound good to you as opposed to those that mirror your audience's search patterns. For instance, a business sells TVs might assume that "best TV" would be a valid keyword, when in reality its customers were mostly searching for things like "cheap TV". Publishers who fail to incorporate keyword research as part of their content creation strategy usually make this mistake. Often, the result is irrelevant content.

It's Simply Not Unique

If your content appears to be a toned-down mash-up of what is available elsewhere on the Internet, then you are merely providing your audience with what they are already tired of seeing. Internet users want something unique, a different perspective on that subject of debate, advice that goes beyond cookie-cutter, or news that is broken first by you. When you are able to provide them with a relatable spectrum of any of these information sets, then you are well set up to scale through their subconscious relevance filter.

The common theme that can be inferred from these signs (and their underlying causes) is that content drummed up without putting the audience in perspective will not appeal to its target audience. If your goal is to get people hooked, you need to know what they want and how they want it presented.

Chapter 9

SOCIAL MEDIA PLATFORMS

Social media is about sociology and psychology more than technology.

Brian Solis

SOCIAL MEDIA IN THE RETAIL INDUSTRY

SOCIAL MEDIA OFFERS RETAILERS AN abundance of information about their customers that they would never be able to get through traditional media.

As social media is a two-way interaction between a person and a brand, by which retailers can understand which of their products buyers like, what brands they prefer, and can get feedback on company service.

Social media has improved the communication link between customers and retailers. The right way to use social media is to create a community that is then helping retailers in the promotion of their business.

Few of the many advantages of social media for retailers are:

* **Contact** – Enquiries and complaints can be sent and answered directly.
* **Loyalty** – Brands created online through social media promotion result in levels of loyalty above the average.
* **Feedback** – Social media will help collect the opinions of users on failed and successful products, including those from competitors.

* **Messaging** – Ability to pass and spread new information quickly or share events that you need to explain and justify.
* **Promotions** – Social media is one of the best places to promote products because of its ability to reach the public in a fast and predictable way.
* **Recommendations** – People tend to search for recommendations of products and services on social networks.

Retailers that genuinely understand the social age will monitor social media and then align their offer to customer needs. When people write negative comments in high quantities about the product, then the brand should seize that opportunity to improve. Similarly, when retailers can seize the opportunity to answer common questions about their brand or products coming from their online community, the retailers can convert those people into fans and ultimately loyal customers.

If retailers are able to build a community around a brand on social media, then when they launch new products or services, they will be able to easily promote it to an existing and loyal community.

Many companies do not want to embrace the power of social media until they know it will bring them positive ROI. That can be a challenge because the social media model is a long-term investment.

A better question to ask is: What is the estimated ROI ten years from now? Or what is the ROI on being relevant to your customers? Social media engagement software can share some insights and metrics, but investment should be long-term.

Social media participation is a long-term investment with hard to calculate ROI. But the industrial age was replaced by the social age, and companies refusing to adapt to the social age will disappear from the market.

By using social media, small companies, when creative, can compete with huge corporations on a much lower budget.

Social Media Impact on the Customer Journey

Foot traffic to brick and mortar stores is falling, despite research showing that people still want to purchase at stores. This fact increases the need for a more significant focus on digital marketing and social media interactions.

The five stages of the buyer journey are:

* Awareness
* Consideration
* Purchase
* Loyalty
* Advocacy

In each of those stages, you can use social media to engage with consumers directly.

Awareness – Can be initiated with a social media post, offline interaction, or an Ad. Consumers go to social media for referrals and recommendations from influencers. Paid social media advertising is important to drive awareness within product categories. Consumers might not be aware of the product as they move into the consideration phase, even if the retailer's brand name is recognizable.

Consideration – When customers need to decide where to make a purchase, they research online. Customers read other customers' reviews, seek other people's opinions, perform Google searches, and search throughout social networks to find a piece of advice on the same product. For your business, it is crucial to have a robust content marketing plan ready that will convince customers to choose your brand. Having old social media without new posts will definitely push customers away. Customers will be even more driven away by social media filled only with commercial posts and links leading to products.

Purchase – Consumers are seeking promotions, and will gladly be driven from social media channels to e-commerce sites or physical stores. In this case, paid social media marketing and shoppable social media links work very well at getting conversions. Social media promotions that motivate customers to visit physical stores will save on delivery costs and potentially increase the total value of sales because customers generally buy more in store than on e-commerce sites.

Loyalty – Ensuring a consistently pleasurable customer experience will create loyalty. Loyalty is key to profitability because the probability of selling to an existing customer is 60–70% while selling to a new customer is 5–20%. Provide fast responses on social media for any customer question, and ensure a fantastic experience via social media. Many brands create fast and efficient customer service via phone or email but fail on social media communication.

Advocacy – The final dream goal for social media in a retail company is advocacy. Nurturing non-paid influencers and users to share your product information and brand messages will reduce the cost of advertising. Social media serves as an effective way to build a bridge between your online e-commerce store and offline stores.

Social Media Platforms for Retailers

Customers will love your product or service more if you also add content that helps them. Consumers use social media to engage with retailers no matter their age, but younger generations have a particular affinity for social media platforms.

Building loyalty among younger generations requires a more personal approach using storytelling and visual aids. They will especially appreciate the ability to interact with brands online and tell them their concerns about products or services.

Retailers can personalize the consumer experience by using social media. A significant number of retailers still think that social media is only a marketing and sales tool. Retailers that use social media only to advertise will damage their long-term goals by failing to use all the other benefits of social media.

Posting content too often or content that is irrelevant to your readers is the same as cold calling. Irrelevant content to your readers is posting only promotional materials. Every fourth post could be something about the product, and three posts should be only about users and what makes them happy.

One of the words in "social media" is "social", so retailers need to engage their customers in some useful way without becoming annoying.

Reasons that people interact with brands online are:

* Enjoying entertaining content
* Giving feedback
* Seeking customer service
* Researching information on the latest products
* Taking advantage of promotions and discounts

When you develop a social strategy or engage with users on social media, you need to take into consideration the reason why they've chosen to interact.

Social media has moved far from being just a promotional channel and, as a retailer, you can either evolve with it or be left behind by competitors.

Here is an overview of social media platforms that are used by retailers.

Pinterest

A platform that should be taken very seriously by any retailer which wants to be successful. Pinterest is a virtual snippet collecting social media site. Brands can use Shoppable Pins to enable users to make direct purchases. While users create themed boards and can upload their own images and products to the board or save brand posts to their lists.

Facebook

At the time of writing, the largest social media site in the world. Excellent platform for brands to market their products and services. Currently, Facebook dominates the digital marketing space and offers outstanding marketing opportunities for retailers. It is essential to understand how often people are using Facebook to interact with businesses. Two-thirds of Facebook users report visiting a local Facebook page a minimum of once a week.

Instagram

The Instagram user base is quickly growing, which was the reason Facebook purchased it. A highly visual platform where users share Stories, live broadcasts, videos, and images. Instagram provides retailers a unique opportunity to showcase their brand because it combines lifting brand awareness, showing off products, and building a community. Instagram gives an excellent opportunity to market your business affordably and is perfect for creative content.

Twitter

A platform that is used as a central exchange between journalists, media, and PR professionals. Twitter is used as an effective communication and opinion exchange platform. It allows users to be on top of trending topics and engage in relevant conversations. Users of Twitter are highly engaged, more so than on other social media networks, despite having fewer users than other platforms.

YouTube

The largest video-sharing social media site in the world, and the second most-visited site in the world. It lets users upload videos on the platform, view videos from others, and interact with them. YouTube is the largest search engine after Google Search. It is a great way to build brand awareness and help your customers to feel connected to your products and services.

LinkedIn

A social media site for professionals with high popularity with the B2B audience. Members use the platform to expand their professional connections, showcase their companies, and search and apply for jobs. A LinkedIn feed is based on the people and topics you want to hear about, so it makes it an excellent place for getting information on matters that affect your business and audience in the short and long term. With the LinkedIn advanced search settings, you can more precisely target the decision-makers.

Snapchat

A highly visual social media platform that is very popular within a new generation of consumers. Users can add statuses on their profiles and send snaps to each other. The core concept of the platform is that any picture or video you send is visible to the recipient for only a short time. It was designed in that way to enable a more natural flow of interaction. The platform itself changes very quickly in terms of functionality, so it might work utterly differently in a few days.

Quora

One of the largest social networks where people ask and answer questions about hundreds of topics and categories. When Google doesn't give you detailed enough customized answers, post it on Quora under a relevant category to get a response. Then you can even send an answer request to topic experts. Quora is a platform where you can connect with people who contribute quality answers, and in that way, build a community around your brand or topic that touches your brand.

Reddit

Social media platform on which users become part of subreddits and engage with others on relevant topics. It became a sort of news aggregators because users share the latest news from different sources. Then others can interact with this news in the form of comments and other interactions. Reddit officially claims that it is "the front page of the Internet," which most users agree with.

WhatsApp

Messaging app that lets users share text messages and many types of files. With the introduction of status features that allow users to update photos or videos, it became a social network and not just a messaging app. On WhatsApp, you can communicate and connect with only the people you want to, and it is used for building business, family, or friend relationships.

WeChat

The most popular social messaging platform in China, where it is possible to do anything from making payments to hailing a ride, or even booking flights. If you would like to attract customers in China or tourists from China, for example, to stores it could be very useful. There are even third-party platforms that can enable you to push your store addresses to WeChat and other useful data to the customers.

Tumblr

Users join communities and cultural dialogues to expand their knowledge and exchange ideas. Tumblr has a reputation for being an anti-blog because of a weak search engine that enables users to be found only by a few friends. Leading social site when it comes to self-expression, often described as a microblog where people usually post short snippets of text and quick snaps, instead of the longer diary-style of blogging. Retailers can use it to quickly launch their website, as it is easy to customize and then use a few of the available advertising options.

Xing

It is a social media site similar to LinkedIn oriented on the European market, predominantly to German-speaking areas. It is not used internationally in any meaningful way. Users can network and create their profiles, so the platform is used more by business professionals. At the time of writing, the platform does not allow the connection of any social media calendar posting software. Therefore, all posts have to be created manually and cannot be pre-arranged, which is something other social media platforms offer.

TikTok

Social Media Platform for creating, sharing, and discovering short music videos. It is used by young people to express their creativity through singing, dancing, comedy, and lip-syncing in videos lasting fifteen seconds or shorter. Younger generations enjoy being more a creator than a spectator, and TikTok enables a fun, creative way for teens, mostly, to express themselves in the form of their own social content.

Google My Business

Google's most successful social platform which was created by taking the already successful service of business listings and slowly adding social features. Users can post and share pictures, write reviews, ask and reply to each other's questions, directly message businesses, and follow them to receive notifications. It might be one of the most important social networks for your business because people who found your listing are already looking to buy what you are selling.

Seven Crucial Social Media Platforms for Retailers

Social media is a necessary part of retail content marketing, so when you start out focus on maintaining a presence on a few channels. After successfully managing those, you can expand onto other platforms after investigating which ones your customers are using.

Below are the best social media networks for retailers beginning social media journeys, together with the best strategies for their use.

* Facebook
* Instagram
* LinkedIn
* Twitter
* Pinterest
* YouTube
* Google My Business

To set up each network, fill your profile with all the necessary information, and make them technically efficient technically: The best way is to read the help section of each network. After opening profiles, reading the help section, and going through the set-up steps, you will understand the network principles better, which will be a good start of your content journey.

Facebook

Facebook is one of the best platforms to reach a larger audience and the largest social media site considering the number of members.

Currently, Facebook dominates the digital marketing space and offers outstanding marketing opportunities for retailers.

The key takeaways to manage the channel successfully are:

* Use analytics for targeting a specific audience and proper timing of the posts. Figure out the best schedules for your posts through trial and error. At: *www.dariosipos.com/resources* you can find some best practice tips on timing.

* When placing ads, adapt them to target specific demographics (locations, age, interests). Make sure that your offer only reaches the people that you intend to target.

* Using lots of images is a great tactic. The chances of a user clicking on your ad increase drastically when you use high-quality images. Here we don't mean a "high-quality resolution," but an image showing fun or useful content.

* Motivate your audience to participate by keeping your posts fun and entertaining. When a post is compelling, it is more likely to be shared.

* Instead of focusing on only getting likes, create pools, or multiple-choice questions. Create questions in such a way that the audience will be motivated to add their vote.

* Focusing solely on your brand will not create a friendly, relatable relationship with the audience. Post some content about other brands that share similar values.

* Where possible, add call to action buttons on your profiles, such as "Message Us", "Shop Now", "Contact Us". Use the call to actions in your posts too.

* Use tools to measure and analyze your Facebook results. Many free tools exist that will give you accurate analytics of what to improve in your posts.

* Create contests to engage the audience and increase brand awareness. This technique is described later in the book.

Retargeting is an essential method for driving ROI on any retail marketing campaign on Facebook. It drives website visitors who did not purchase during their first visit back to your site. A Facebook business page is the most important place for you, from here you can offer special promotions, post images, or post company announcements.

A short checklist of things every retail business Facebook page should have is:

* Customized URL
* Welcome message to direct first time visitors to your page
* List of all your other social media profiles
* Complete informative "About" section with your overall business information, awards, achievements, and your brand story
* All business locations listed if you have more than one
* Customized chat messages, and answering service for any customer questions

When you analyze posts on Facebook, which have successful user engagement, you will notice that they are usually regarding:

* Contests
* Popular culture
* Influencer promotions

Contests are the best way to nurture engagement and build brand awareness and, especially on Facebook, they are effective. More details on how to manage contests for promotion is available in chapter 10, in the section: Methodology of Promoting Retail Online.

Niche Facebook Groups are an excellent spot for any retailer to market their products and bring awareness to their brand. Although niche groups already contain an audience that is very interested in certain products, it's necessary not to be aggressive with promotion. A better method is to take part in discussions and offer solutions only when they are visibly needed.

Some Groups are explicitly made for promotions; on them, you can be an active member, offer promotions, or hand out discount codes.

Any retailer, even with a limited budget, can run retargeting campaigns that will result in high ROI, using these steps:

1. Run a contest.
2. Convince users to tag their friends and share the content.

3. Promote product pages on your site through this contest.
4. Finish contest.
5. Re-target the users that visited you with discounts or other promotions.

Managing the marketing of retail products on Facebook is a daily task that needs to be done systematically, because trends are continually changing and Facebook quite often changes how users can see your messages.

Instagram

Instagram has become a crucial marketing and sales opportunity for retailers, especially in regards to the younger generation. It is parallelly often described as a holy grail for small retailers due to its ability to drive sales on a low budget while being scalable.

The key takeaways to manage the channel successfully are:

* Instagram is primarily an image sharing site, which means that you need to focus on your visuals. Offer visually likable content that is interesting.

* Use Instagram stories because they are entertaining, habit creating, and you can easily personalize it to your brand by simply showing what you are doing behind the scenes daily.

* Instagram is very well accepted between employees, especially of the younger generation. Therefore, you can significantly support employee participation.

* IGTV (Instagram TV) gives you a longer format so you can present products or unboxing videos. Significant brands shoot videos unboxing and testing products.

* Posting often is essential. It is crucial to stay active and give it more attention than some other channels may require.

* Communicate with people, engage with them. People will like your content because you like their content.

* Products need to be shown through engaging content, which does not focus only on sales. Eye-catching images are essential: Instagram is fundamentally a platform where customers search for purchase inspiration.

* Use hashtags to target your customers and subjects your ideal customer might be interested in.
* Create your own hashtags and engage with people to encourage its use.
* Find the perfect timing by using some free online software to see which tags and filters have the best correlation to comments on posts.
* To reach a specific audience among such a great number of people using the platform, use hashtags, mentions, sponsored ads, and stories.

The reason that Instagram is such an excellent tool for your business is that it uses photos as a primary way of communication. Photos are the best thing in marketing for reasons because they:

* Make your company brand more relatable
* Are engaging
* Make way more emotional connection than just text

User-generated content is an excellent method to build a community around your brand. So do your best to convince followers to submit their own photos, which you can then feature on your feed or Instagram Story.

One of the major ways to be successful on Instagram is to create your own original content and then consistently share it with your followers.

Instagram is no doubt a strong marketing tool, but it also contains tools that will enable any retailer to grow sales. One such tool is the option of a shoppable post. When your account is approved through a simple process, you can tag your products in images and videos so your viewers can buy them directly in the application. Other tools such as using product stickers in Instagram Stories also boost sales.

On Instagram, content is everything, so to make your brand stand out using the following methods:

* Posting consistently and frequently to grab viewers' attention.
* Visually attractive posts will attract more attention.
* Create a theme for the Instagram brand page, through color, pattern, and filters.

* Speak with a tone of communication that matches your audience.
* Invest plenty of effort in writing captions and researching hashtags.

Instagram stories are images and videos that users can upload, which disappear after some time if not saved permanently to a profile. Sponsored ads can be promoted through stories, which is a very effective method of promotion. Using as many features as possible on Instagram stories will make content more engaging.

When managing stories, the best results will have:
* A length of fifteen seconds (as a most effective ad format)
* Questions and pooling features to drive engagement
* Announcements or new products
* Stickers and emojis to create more exciting content
* A consistent timeline of daily posts
* A set of important stories saved with the "highlights" so they are permanently visible

Using the paid option of sponsored ads can build recognition and are simple to use while being highly effective. When paying for ads, you can choose the demographics, location, age, area, and interest of the users you target. Those ads will then drive the user to a page or website through a direct link in them.

Influencer marketing, a modern-day version of word-of-mouth marketing, is one of the most essential ways of making your brand visible on Instagram.

Some advice on influencer marketing on Instagram:
* Choosing a few smaller micro-influencers (followers up to 10,000) is better than one macro influencer (above 100,000 followers).
* Build your team of influencers that will be loyal to your brand, instead of changing between many influencers.
* Connect with the right type of influencers based on categories you want to cover.
* The quality of content that influencers can produce is a significant factor influencing KPI.

More details on how to manage influencers are available in chapter 10, in the section: Methodology of Promoting Retail Online.

When you create a strong visual brand on Instagram, build a community around it, and start using all social selling options available, then your business will get strong engagement, a more significant community, and an increase in sales.

LinkedIn

LinkedIn is a great platform to grow your business, next to being a platform for professionals and job seekers. On LinkedIn, you can make connections, generate leads, build brand awareness, and significantly contribute to your company's digital marketing strategy. LinkedIn requires a different approach to other social media platforms because the method of pushing your business with sales messages won't work. Mostly this is because LinkedIn is built of a different audience than other social networks.

The key takeaways to manage this channel successfully are:

* Fill your company profile and personal profile entirely until they are marked "All-Star".

* Have an updated and consistent presence for your brand on the company profile page. All materials should be consistent with your website and any other social media profiles that you operate. The page should be updated regularly.

* Targeting on LinkedIn is unmatched on any other digital advertising platform. A retailer can zero in on the specific industry and company size that would typically buy their product or be their supplier.

* If you wish to purchase goods for your outlet or are a wholesaler, you can convince any supplier in any part of the world that you are their ideal buyer or distributor for your country. Instead of visiting trade fairs, you can do your supplier search much faster through LinkedIn and, even better, enable suitable suppliers to find you around the clock.

* Post high-quality content that will be highly targeted by merely being excellent and relevant to the audience. Content should teach others how to solve the problem or be better at some task, which will establish you as a thought leader.

* Writing articles on LinkedIn is a powerful way of promoting your company.
* Convince your employees to create their profiles on LinkedIn. They should be filled entirely, including all their job histories and proper photos, because it will help your business grow.
* Joining LinkedIn Groups relevant to your target demographic is a great way to conduct social listening and interact with other business owners, suppliers, or random companies from which you can learn something useful. By using the LinkedIn InMail function, you can contact anyone building a valuable relationship with a new supplier.
* Use the platform regularly, publish content, and also engage with the content of your strategic partners and suppliers every day.

LinkedIn is a social network for professionals to connect with other professionals easily. That means as a retail business, you can connect with strategic partners, other business owners, and suppliers. Once you create connections, you can nurture them to become great relationships.

Twitter

Twitter is used more as a news source or news feed than a marketing channel, so to get high traffic to your website it's necessary to share quality content.

Twitter is the primary channel for journalists and media and is very popular in the USA, UK, and gradually in other countries too.

The key takeaways to manage this channel successfully are:

* Show off your best sales and promotions, because many customers go to Twitter to search for big sales.
* Use free analytics to measure your growth and find where users are.
* Twitter users have higher shopping budgets than other platforms and generally shop more, so use it for marketing higher-priced goods.
* Twitter claims the highest ROI for retailers that use it for marketing.

* Ads use on Twitter is growing and is different from other social media in that the costs have decreased.
* Use hashtags to get to the top of feeds, and use popular hashtags for new positioning.
* Run a contest to increase engagement, as Twitter and its hashtags are ideal for creating a network around contests.
* Create Twitter-specific offers so that people can only access by following your brand on Twitter.

Many types of research show that Twitter is essential for retailers that are looking to communicate with their customer base.

The primary use of Twitter in retail is that users share their experiences, ideas, and thoughts through the platform. Users on Twitter will quickly and honestly tell you if your customer service is excellent and commercial offer reasonable. Don't forget to join the conversation by retweeting, replying, or saving favorite comments. In the case of negative comments, apologize, and use the guide available in chapter 10, in the section: Methodology of Promoting Retail Online on how to handle negative feedback.

Twitter advertising options revolve around flexible options that align with retailer goals, such as:
* New followers
* Engagements or app installations
* Website clicks or conversions
* Leads on Twitter
* Tweet engagement (favorites, retweets, replies)

Of those, website click campaigns are the most useful for a retailer. To be successful, listen to your audience, respond, and connect with them. Provide valuable information, service, and use ads to create conversion.

Pinterest

Pinterest is a powerful virtual corkboard and the ultimate platform for searching for inspiration and planning projects. Most users know it as a visual discovery tool and a catalog of ideas. Any content you make should not be disruptive to the user's experience. People that visit Pinterest are looking for inspiration and ideas.

It is highly recommended that you read the user manual help section of Pinterest because it explains in a simple way how to operate the platform to maximum effect.

The key takeaways to manage the channel successfully are:

* Pinterest is more than just a social network. It contains its own powerful search engine. Map out the keywords that are important for you. When you post a picture by creating a pin, you will need to write text to accompany it, including mapped keywords and hashtags.

* Paying for promoted pins will increase your brand exposure instantly. Post organic pins but also use paid pins to highlight your best performing organic posts.

* Pinterest enables a few types of campaigns. Engagement campaigns will increase the number of saves for a post. Traffic campaigns will bring customers to a website to create sales. An awareness campaign will display your content to as many users as possible and attract new customers.

* Target your audience by micro-targeting by demographics, because it will increase sales conversions. Pinterest has a much higher average purchase order than other social media networks.

* To enable purchases made directly through Pinterest use Buyable Pins. Even though purchases are made directly through Pinterest, you can still set up your shipping and customer guidelines. Mix shoppable pins with other pins to attract a larger audience and to not irritate customers with too many sales-oriented pins.

* Focus on creating excellent content because Pinterest is about smooth gliding through relevant content.

* Posts need to be optimized for mobile because 82% of users are on the mobile app.

* Pinterest can be used very effectively to acquire early shoppers around the holiday seasons: Pinterest users are people that plan far in advance.

* Create boards that include a mix of Buyable Pins and non-Buyable Pins to show the uses of your shoppable products.

You will have the best results when you create themed boards that are a mixture of inspirational Pins and not only shoppable products. In that way, you will create an organic targeted audience that will save and purchase specific Pins.

Pinterest is a virtual ideas environment, and once you learn more about the platform, then you will make sure success. You will increase brand awareness by pinning stunning images and also attract new customers by using Pins to serve them as ideas with useful information.

YouTube

As one of the first social media channels that came into existence, YouTube is not only a place to watch videos but it is also the second-largest search engine in the world.

YouTube is an effective channel to build brand awareness and connect your target customers to your brand. If you can create interesting content, then you have more chances to create engagement. The benefit of YouTube over traditional media, such as TV, is that you can create good enough content even with your phone camera.

The key takeaways to manage the channel successfully are:

* When you create videos, they should always be one of these three types: Entertaining, Educational, or Inspiring.
* Consistency is crucial both in terms of regularity and posting time. Posting videos once a week is vital to be successful. Consistency will enable your audience to expect and see videos at the same time, according to a preannounced schedule.
* Create videos of an ideal length of three to four minutes, any longer and the audience will lose interest.
* Create videos in advance, so you will always stick to your video publishing calendar. Consistently demonstrate your value and strive to have a smart and straightforward video that makes a great story but based on a simple concept.
* Once when you have a video of longer duration, make short thirty-second trailers out of it and post them on other platforms.

In that way, you can repurpose the video on other social media channels and still drive viewers to see it on YouTube.

* Always use consistent branding on YouTube and across your other channels. Don't try experiments that are very different to your usual branding or promise what you cannot deliver.

* Investing in equipment is a good idea, especially when it comes to sound, lighting, and editing software. All of the mentioned investments are small compared to any typical retail investment.

* Growing a large, engaged audience takes time and consistent effort, so get ready for it by creating and writing down your long-term strategy without expecting sudden success. Decide on why you are creating videos. Is it to increase brand awareness, or to increase sales or to show customers how products work? Decide on a theme and key messages.

* The section below the video is a precious place to add your links or a coupon code for sales. Including descriptions, other channels, or information on how to contact you is crucial.

* YouTube has its own search engine optimization ranking algorithm, which is similar to Google. Using keywords, titles, hashtags, and writing a good description will help generate more traffic.

Videos represent an extraordinary opportunity for success on social media. Years ago, you would require a team of professionals and a huge budget to create a single video, but today you can create it by using a phone camera combined with some user-friendly editing software. In that way, you can create great looking and meaningful videos in-house for a fraction of the cost and compete successfully with large brands.

Google My Business

Social networks are so crucial in today's society; Google has launched eight social networks, most of which were shut down. The most famous of those that were discontinued was Google+.

The most used and most popular Google social network is currently Google My Business. As it is a business-related social network, it is crucial for any retailer.

Many readers will be surprised that Google My Business is included here as a social network, but the reason will become clearer as we cover the services it offers:

* Listings – Businesses can create a listing with its location, opening hours, and other details.
* Reviews – Users can write reviews for businesses
* Following – Users can follow a business to receive notifications.
* Posts – Businesses can share videos and pictures.
* Questions – Users and businesses can ask and answer each other questions.
* Messaging – Users can directly message businesses.
* Special Offers – Businesses can send special offers.
* Special Invites – Users can get exclusive event invites.

Based on all of those features, we can definitely consider Google My Business to be a social networking site.

The key takeaways to manage the channel successfully are:

* If you, as a retailer, operate multiple locations, then it is necessary to create a listing for each location and link them together as all belonging to you.
* Create content formatted according to the needs and questions of users.
* Post content (images, posts, offers) regularly because posts are valid for only seven days.
* Monitor your listings every day, and respond to questions and reviews (either positive or negative).
* Assign one team member to actively respond to reviews, and make sure there are no delays.
* Regularly read Google updates on the platform to keep up with current trends and possible changes in the way the platform works.
* Use Google My Business together with Google Search Console to check what your users are searching for and their content interests, then simply manufacture matching content.

Google My Business is possibly one of the most important social networks for you as a retailer because of the marketing funnel structure.

Social media belongs on top of the sales funnel because there you engage users to convince them that your brand or products are worth their attention. That process of convincing users costs you a significant amount of time and money.

Search engine marketing is considered the bottom of the sales funnel because users are already closer to a purchase. It is not necessary to convince users that they need your product, as they are already actively searching for a product that you are offering.

That makes Google My Business an incredibly important social network for your business because people who have found your listing are probably local customers already searching for what you are offering.

All retailers should be paying close attention to all the features of Google My Business, as it will enable their company to stand out in search results.

GROWTH MARKETING

Growth marketing is a mixture of marketing, sales, customer success, support, and other operations in your organization. It is also an approach to growing your business and optimizing content marketing as a consequence of continuous testing across marketing channels.

Each channel has its own advertising system. To learn how each channel functions, the best method is to read the help section of each platform or visit one of many available free classes online.

Content creators continuously fight for the attention of users. The Artificial Intelligence of search engines is now capable of interpreting searches to find pages that actually don't have the exact words that people searched for. This is done by the search engine by associating search history with similar themes, and it means your business can be found online by their ideal audience.

It is essential not to forget that you are not creating content only for search engines because your actual customer is human being.

Creating compelling content means that you will be able to create a positive user experience that works for both the searcher and the search engine, not just one or the other.

When planning a social media strategy include the following as mandatory:

1. There should be only a business strategy and not a social media strategy. Then social media activities should be aligned with business strategy.
2. Social media use at work should be fully allowable at all times, and employees should be encouraged to support the company online. Ask every single employee to help the company online: Inform them about new products via social media, and ask them to share your company updates. Use social media to engage with employees that support you online, on platforms where they are now.
3. Employees will value a lot a free social media training, therefore provide it to them and include how they can support the company online.
4. There should be an exchange collaboration platform, like Slack or Microsoft Teams which are similar to social media networks, in place because it will make your team more productive.
5. When planning on which social media platform to engage with customers, meet customers where they are now. It will be Facebook, Twitter, LinkedIn, or others, depending on your region.
6. Use social media to engage with your outside partners and suppliers on platforms on which they are present. Usually, this will be business format networks like LinkedIn or Xing. Find and follow, like, and engage with the content of your suppliers. They will soon return you a favor and become your loyal social media supporters.
7. Make your CEO's social presence strong. He should be active and have a strong position online. Presence needs to be "social" instead of "PR &Media." Never make your social

media just another channel for your PR and marketing department.

8. Create thought leaders online; your CEO should be a thought leader, so should your digital manager and sales director. They should have a strong presence and be active on a few platforms, and at least on LinkedIn and Twitter.

9. When creating the online presence of employees, don't worry about company ranks and positions. Employees who love and know social media are rare, and you need to make them be your social superstars that will promote your brand online.

10. Create testimonials from existing customers and use them online. Customers do research online, so all references online need to be really good. Social media channels are the best ways to communicate, identify, and solve customer problems. Create content that answers frequently asked questions.

11. The sales team communicates with customers (existing, and potential). And they interact with customers who decide to quit doing business with you because they do not like your service. The sales team has valuable information on which content will help bring more customers. Use their knowledge to get feedback on what content is right.

12. If your company operates in the B2B arena as well as the retail arena, which is quite common, then make sure your company and salespeople have good profiles on business professionals' networks, for example, LinkedIn. Because a proper online presence of a company and salesperson will help them make initial contact with new B2B customers and open doors for them before they even arrive at the meeting. Most salespeople in B2B agree that the hardest challenge is creating that first contact or meeting.

13. Have a reliable social media customer service plan in place. When customers contact you on social media, with a complaint about a product or service, answer immediately to demonstrate to others how you take care of your users'

problems. Define answering times for members of your team, and create a process for handling customer complaints arriving through social media networks.

14. Connect sincerely with everyone possible online. Search for journalists and other influencers and then connect with them too.

Social media platforms offer numerous benefits, including promotional and PR power.

It is important to stress that your biggest supporters on social media, and generally online, should be your employees. They can create the first engagement with your content in the form of likes and shares, and most of them will be more than happy to support their company. First likes on a post and early engagement are the hardest to get, so that can be solved by the support of your employees.

Chapter 10

PROMOTING CONTENT EFFICIENTLY

Before you create any more 'great content', figure out how you are going to market it first.

Joe Pulizzi

IMPORTANCE OF CONTENT PROMOTION

CONTENT PROMOTION ENSURES THAT CONTENT will reach its intended targets. If the content which you create is going to bring you benefits, then you need to have people actually read it. Therefore, your content promotion strategy is of the same value as content creation.

You need to create great content so you can acquire high-quality off-site signals, which will be interpreted by search engines as brand and industry authority, and eventually will lead to visibility. If you do not have a broad audience, then even superior content has to be pushed to be discovered. Content promotion is crucial for bringing your content to new online audiences and eventually earn you the traffic and conversions, which is your ultimate SEO goal.

Content promotion is crucial for SEO, as it is one of the search engine ranking factors. Here are the ways that search engines interpret content promotion:

* **Social signals** – Making your content be viewed by the right audience via the right channel. When that content is interesting for the viewers, it will drive engagement via social channels.

* **Earned links** – Earned links as a result of the promoted content that has value for its audience are very valuable.
* **Improved domain authority and rankings** – Social signals and earned links drastically increase search rankings and domain authority. When creating and promoting good content, this will indicate that you are successful.
* **Increased web traffic and conversions** – Higher organic search rankings will bring higher traffic and higher conversions. Content promotion and SEO are interconnected, where success in one will create success in the others.
* **Off-site signals** – when traffic and conversions increase, then your content will be visible to a bigger audience. This will result in more links, traffic, engagement, conversions, and higher rankings.

Content that brands create should position them as thought leaders, but not as a hero in the eyes of their customers. Increased off-site signals increase domain authority and search visibility. To earn these signals, it is necessary to create and promote content that is valuable enough to be shared.

There are a variety of channels where you can do content promotion, and new ones appear often. Channels for content promotion can be email, webinars, social media networks, blogs, and others. Opportunities to promote content are endless, and you should base them around your regular company operation and build them into company fabric.

Naturally, you should publish your content on Facebook, but also you should spend significant time finding out where your current and potential customers spend time online.

Content promotion needs to be used in order to reach a new audience and connect your business with them: If you do not reach new audiences, you cannot grow your audience. For example, if you manage your Instagram account by merely publishing content to existing followers without reaching a new audience, then your follower count will stay low forever.

Content promotion brings website traffic, improves engagement, and convinces potential customers to do business with you. It will help to communicate the value you provide and to nurture relationships, creating word-of-mouth promotions in turn.

Each channel has its own advertising system. To learn how each channel functions, the best method is to read the help section of each platform or visit one of many available free classes online. All the platforms contain help sections that will guide you on how to successfully use them, especially in regards to paid promotions.

One of the more significant ways companies make a mistake when trying to make digital transformations is that they send their team members to local classes organized by local marketing agencies, which teach them how to do proper advertising online. That education is often outdated, based on the personal opinion of instructors and their limited business experience in the real field of work. All materials on how to do promote content are available online. Most of the materials teaching you how to use a social platform are contained within the platform in the format of their user manual or even video guides.

As a retailer, it is crucial that you get your education from multiple sources but always strive to get it directly from the platform owner. No person will be able to tell you better which data entry fields need to be filled in the Facebook Business Page than Facebook itself.

ORGANIC AND PAID CONTENT PROMOTION

It's essential is to understand the differences between organic and paid promotions and how they influence each other.

Before diving into these subjects, let's summarize all five types of media where you, as a company, can promote a brand or product.

1. **Paid Media** – Advertising, such as magazine advertising, sponsored content, display ads, PPC ads, price comparators, and other types.
2. **Earned Media** – Looks like traditional public relations, resulting from public, media, blogging, and influencer methods of promotion.

3. **Owned Media** – Media that you own, ranging from blogs and your website to papers: The main focus of your content marketing efforts.

4. **Shared Media** – Shared content, referrals, community-driven content, reviews, and, where the first three overlap, promoted brand content, sponsored customers, and brands that ask for shares.

5. **Converged Media** – All of the above four categories combined and integrated create a new type of promotion. It is less about media, but more about cross channel integration.

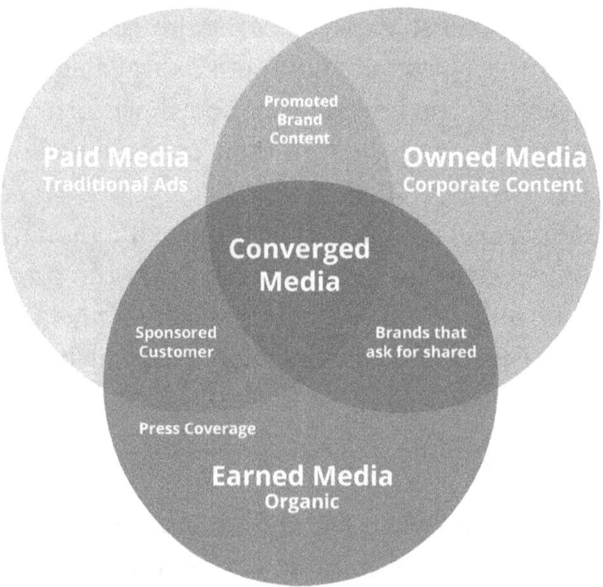

Figure 3. The Converged Media Imperative: How Brands Must Combine Paid, Owned & Earned Media, Source: Altimeter Group, 2012.

No single type of medium can stand alone and be successful. Therefore, it is essential to converge all types of media.

The customer journey is always cross channel and never linear. Therefore, the dynamic customer journey needs to be taken into consideration. In the center of the customer-centric view stands the fact that no medium or channel should be disconnected, which is different from a channel-by-channel view because our content, media, and channels merely serve as a way to accomplish business goals. The main factor driving all our efforts should be actual customer experience and every point of contact with our business, no matter of types of media and channels that create it.

Good marketing is always integrated marketing.

Organic content promotion increases the visibility of your content and the efficiency of your marketing campaigns without spending money on ads.

Just a few of the most effective organic content promotion methods are:

* Web pages, articles and blogs entries
* Guest blogs
* Email marketing
* Webinars
* Influencers
* Videos
* How-to guides
* Case studies
* Infographics
* Customer reviews
* Streaming presentation
* User Generated content
* Interviews
* Customer support stories

The benefit of doing organic promotion is creating your brand authority on many potential platforms. Because you do not need a budget to do organic promotion, then you have no limitations to promote more.

Increasing brand awareness is one of the crucial benefits of your organic promotion. Consistency plays a vital role in promoting your content, both for brand recognition and satisfying social media and search engine algorithms.

One of the main channels for paid promotions is search engine ads on search platforms and paid social media campaigns on social media.

Paid promotions are best to deliver highly targeted content to the public that will find your content useful. Paid promotions depend on budgets to achieve results. Testing is essential at first in paid promotions, in order not to waste your budget on poorly performing paid campaigns.

The best results for your company will be achieved when you use paid promotion on your best performing organic content. So, bringing both types of promotions together will bring you the best results.

On search engine pages, such as Google, it is harder to choose which is good content to promote. Therefore, you need to check what performs well and then decide whether to promote it. Social media platforms will propose paid promotion on high performing organic content.

Promoting content should attract new users to your pages. If you are not getting new users to your pages, that is a reliable indicator that promotion is not performing well.

Customizing messages for each channel is essential, always test the performance of promoting content on a smaller budget, before you invest a more substantial sum.

Outperforming at Content Promotion

Being excellent at content promotion requires serious work, and some strategies are proven to work the best.

Make a general social media calendar for your company and include details of your targets, all channels, and types of content that will be created.

Then also use a social media calendar, such as Buffer or Hootsuite, that will create consistency in your content publishing schedule.

In paid campaigns, you can target specific audiences down to the smallest detail. When doing organic promotion, you have to create imagined targeting, create different kinds of posts depending on various purposes and possible audiences.

Create a customized message on each channel while offering value. Each post should be an invitation for your audience to either engage with your business or to build a relationship with it by creating trust.

Naturally, in each country, a retailer needs to experiment with its content and, by testing, determine what works best.

When creating posts of any type, follow this proven formula:

* Publish ten posts promoting content from a third-party website, which will help you increase credibility as an information hub for your industry.
* Publish four posts promoting original content created by your business. Blogs, videos or anything to show your reader that you can provide original useful content.
* Publish one post supporting an offer on your products, where you are positioned as a guide.

Analyzing the promotion of your channel results is essential. Check which post message had the highest achievement. Then include findings in the next campaigns. As mentioned, the best results will be achieved if you do paid promotion on content that already performed best organically.

MEASURING AND READING RESULTS

To see if your posts and all your efforts are liked beyond your company, it is crucial to measure and analyze the results of your campaigns. Measuring is essential to see if you need to adjust your future content.

Compared to traditional marketing, with digital content marketing it is even harder to see results. Many results arrive later and are not visible immediately.

Measures that can be tracked in your campaigns include:

1. Brand awareness
2. Engagement
3. Lead generation
4. Customer loyalty and retention
5. Customer conversion and sales
6. Website performance

Let's dive deeper into each measure.

Brand Awareness

This is a parameter that can push you both to the top of search engines and to be the first idea in your customer's head when they think about some product you offer.

Brand awareness can mean more things in the digital world: social media followers, backlinks to your posts, reach depending on the channel, conversations about a brand (mentions on social media, reviews). In search engines, it can be how many people are searching for you or how many have your webpage bookmarked in their browser, or how many are entering your address directly as a URL without doing research. Traffic to the site also indicates that your brand is high ranking in brand awareness.

Google Alerts will be an effective way of getting notified whenever your brand gets mentioned online. It will inform you via email that someone mentioned you in their posts, articles, or other media.

Tactics for measuring brand awareness can be:

Surveys – Conducting a survey by email or website asking a random selection of people if they are familiar with your brand.

Direct website traffic – Direct Channel in Google Analytics tracks the number of people who typed your URL into their address bar or used a bookmark. Monitoring this traffic will indicate if your brand awareness changes over time.

Search volume data – Using Google Trends or Google AdWords Keyword Planner to check the volume of searches for your brand name and its changes over time.

Social listening – Allows you to listen online for organic conversations about your brand across all the channels. It is a significantly better method than surveys because it eliminates response bias.

Engagement

Engagement means measuring how many users interact with your content. This parameter will be important in the case of "likes" disappearing from social networks. Likes going away from social networks is an idea that will become a reality sooner or later. Instead of Likes, there is a set of other parameters that social networks will depend on more.

Engagement on social media is a sum of comments, likes, shares, and retweets. Engagement is also when your readers click on your email mailing campaign or them forwarding your email to their friends.

Lead Generation

A proper way to prove that your company resources are spent on a good purpose is measuring lead generation. Measurements can include how many leads you generate, for example, new users subscribing to your newsletters.

Discovering which specific action that you made pushed someone to become a lead can generate a recipe for getting more leads. For example, finding out what made leads become your newsletter subscribers is valuable information that you can use for the future.

Customer Loyalty and Retention

Tracking how often customers buy from you or if they recommend you to others is valuable information for your future efforts. Whether customers are returning or only transacting onetime is important information, particularly if the cost of acquisition is high, so you can focus your efforts on where it counts.

Customer Conversion and Sales

Here you determine what is good ROI on your content marketing process, or the actual cost for the acquisition of a new customer. Check what the ratio of leads to customers is then, based on data, connect your marketing efforts properly with your sales team.

Website Performance

To measure your website performance, measure traffic including unique visitors and pageviews and which sources of traffic are top-performing. If one channel brings more customers, then focus the budget on that channel to increase sales.

Check how channels perform organically. They must bring more organic customers over time. Search engines will judge your page for quality based on the number of organic visitors. Organic visitors arrive based on your high-quality content. Therefore, search engines think that the more organic visitors you have, the higher-quality content you have.

APPLYING DATA

When you collect data, share it with your full team, including the sales team and management. Use data for updating your goals and your content process. Creating an explanation of your data is very important, so you can convince the rest of your team to work on common goals.

Have regular meetings with your teams to explain the results and create an action plan for improvement of each segment through content.

Data on your organic efforts and brand awareness compared to the competition, benchmarked over time, can be collected using various online software solutions. New solutions are appearing regularly, so it's best to compare a few current solutions by doing online research and check which one matches the volume of your business the best.

At the time of writing, some of the popular and best solutions include Alexa by Amazon (*www.alexa.com*) or SEMrush (*www.semrush.com*) or SimilarWeb (*www.similarweb.com*). These solutions differ by pricing and functionality, so at the beginning of your efforts it is enough to use a low-cost solution without advanced functions.

It is important to note that if you are checking your organic growth in Google Analytics, then you are seeing changes compared only to your own previous period. Effectively it means that while your organic growth may be great, it may be that the competition is growing faster organically. So, use the tools mentioned above to see how you compare to competitors and gain some improvement ideas from the software.

METHODOLOGY OF PROMOTING RETAIL ONLINE

We will name some of the ideas for adapting your daily processes to be used in your content efforts online. Also, in this section are answers to most commonly asked questions and concerns about online content, based on my experience of working with retailers.

Every retailer already has enough promotional material, events, and excitement in their daily work to use it for online content. What is missing is most likely just some slight adaptation of the available material for online use. Such as documenting what the company does in daily work, and then mentioning it online on their social media channels and platforms.

For example, every meeting that you have with a supplier should be photographed and then posted on social media with an interesting description of the event. Just add a little bit of creativity in writing, and you have an interesting social media post.

Social Media Influencers

Influencer marketing is one of the most necessary items on your list of necessities for your retail business promotion, and it is, in principle, supercharged word-of-mouth.

Social influencers are most often categorized by their audience size. For a retail promotion, it's best to use micro-influencers, which are classified as an influencer with under 100,000 followers on social media. By experience, we know that it is better to have a few smaller influencers, with each having 5,000 – 10,000 followers on social media, than one bigger influencer.

Few smaller micro-influencers can be spread through different categories of products that you sell on a smaller budget than one famous influencer. For example, one influencer can cover the fitness category, and others can cover cooking, car accessories, or any other category of products where you need to create branding for your business.

Small micro-influencers will enable you to reach a more targeted audience. So, you can use even a few small micro-influencers in the same campaign to reach more people.

It is better to work with a small influencer that has real influence in some category or sphere of human life. An important factor is the influencer's relevancy to your business/niche/category, and if their audience is your target audience.

When searching for an influencer, first decide which categories of products are essential to be promoted for your business and then use common sense to locate appropriate influencers on the social media platform. You want an influencer that will not control you, or cost you too much, but will behave as a partner with you.

After you locate an influencer and make a deal with them, make sure you sign an agreement by which your influencer will actively promote you on all possible channels and post content themselves, instead of only delivering materials to you.

Most of the great successful campaigns actually focus on smaller micro-influencers or even regular people because authenticity is the most crucial factor on social media.

Discussion Forums and Social Media Groups

Across the Internet, there are various discussion forums and social media groups divided by niche, and many of them are in the local language of the country where you operate.

One way to reach a wider community for your social media or your blogs is by inserting a link to them on other possible places, such as customer forums, social media groups, and comment sections on other news sites. Naturally, you should contribute to actual discussion and not merely insert a link to your website or social media.

Check for social media groups on specific topics that your buyer's persona might be interested in and then add your content advising people that they can benefit from visiting your site or social media.

When you hire micro-influencers to promote your brand or products, make sure that they post content all over social media channels, specialized groups, and discussion forums also by participating in real conversations.

Sponsorships

As a retailer, you are often asked to sponsor events, festivals, or sports teams. One of the dimensions you should add to your usual sponsorship deal is to include a social media component.

Instead of financially sponsoring an event for which you were asked to sponsor, it's better to create public polls a few times per year asking the public who they would like you to sponsor.

For example, instead of sponsoring a music festival that was offered to you, create an open call and ask your social media followers which music festival they would like to see you sponsor.

Do that much in advance before the planned event, and when you get a general idea, ask your followers again to vote between a few more narrowed-down choices. Go to discussion forums and social media groups and ask users there the same question. In this way, instead of passively handing out money, you will engage with the public and bring more followers to your brand. Such a way of working can give you months of content material, where your followers will engage with your brand and push engagement up significantly.

Charity Work

Social media is an ideal medium to bring awareness to a charity or cause that your company cares about or already sponsors. It will help to show more transparency as to where your funds are going and target your help to people or organizations where your donation will be most useful.

Each year, you can ask your followers if they know some worthy cause that would benefit from financial aid or packages of goods specially designed by your business for the charity. For example, you could dedicate part of the profits of a specific line to charity, which is a great way to help that will be much appreciated by your followers.

Social Media Contests

One of the fantastic ways to engage with your audience, build a community, or raise awareness is to create social media contests. Instead of spending money on social media ads, you can run a contest organically and regularly give some prizes. Even low-cost rewards, for example, cheap headphones or cheap blenders, will attract and engage people more than social media paid ads. Contests can be a simple giveaway of a small valued item or more extensive campaign with big prizes.

Social media contests provide value by boosting brand or product awareness, increasing your social following, engaging the community, creating user generated content, and growing your email subscriber list.

Before you run your contest, decide which of the values and goals mentioned above are most important to your business. Currently, the best contests are done on Facebook and Instagram, which naturally means you should research your platforms before you run your contests.

The steps to running successful contests are:
* Setting goals and budget
* Choosing prizes and the reason why customers will join (is a prize worth their effort?)
* Choose a social network and contest type
* Decide on the frequency and length of the contest
* Define legal requirements
* Promote and help participants engage
* Convert participants to be your brand ambassadors and analyze achievements

Some examples of contests are:
* Cooking recipe contest
* Photo contest
* Caption contest
* Sweepstakes
* Like, share and reply
* Vote to win
* Video contests

University or School Lectures and Conferences
One of the highest levels of organic positioning you can achieve is by cooperating with schools and universities. This will boost your brand awareness among the younger generation, and it is a perfect opportunity to use it on your social media channels. Cooperation can be by holding a lecture for students or bringing students to visit your company. Before and after, you need to use social media to announce, promote, and report from the event. Ask the students to help you post

content from their visit or lecture to social media. Publishing a short article on the University or School webpage with a link to your company will create valuable organic backlinks.

Participating in conferences can position you as a thought leader and bring up awareness of your brand and company achievements.

Instead of only *participating* in conferences, an even better idea is to create your own conference or event. Events do not need to be large or fancy, and you can create a free event for the public and use social media to promote it.

PR Announcements

Most of the retailers are still using PR announcements as a method of informing the public about their achievements. The usual way involves sending PR announcements to their favorite marketing agency, which then distributes it to local media. Despite PR announcements having low effects online, compared to other methods of spreading the word, there are still effective ways to use the Internet to send PR announcements.

There are specialized companies online and, at this current moment, one of the best solutions is called PR Underground, which will enable sending PR announcements adapted to the online environment. Such solutions include PR, Social Media, and SEO all in one. So, it is a particular version of social media press releases that will often end up on Google News, get distributed to social media, and published on a minimum of 80+ news sites. At any given moment, you can research for currently available similar solutions online. This method is also available at a much lower cost than traditional PR.

Hashtags

A keyword or phrase preceded by a hash sign (#) is used within a post on social media to help people interested in a certain topic to find you when they search for a keyword or particular hashtag. New brand identity and awareness can be created by proper hashtag use. Hashtags are effective tools in the form of communication, for example on Instagram, which is an image-oriented platform.

Next to creating your own hashtag connected with your brand and company name, there are others that you can create to boost your chances of showing up in search results. For example, you can generate a hashtag for the specific purpose of being connected with your brand, in the form of some motivating short buzzword.

The best hashtags will always describe your customer's lifestyle and interests, and never your product attributes. Use situations or places where your customer would use your product to create a hashtag that will describe that situation.

Responding to Reviews and Comments

All reviews or comments on your social media accounts should be responded to promptly, no matter if they are positive or negative, to show your brand followers how much you care about their feedback or requests for help. Word-of-mouth is effective, so social media reviews and comments can attract customers to you or push them away. Customers will read your response to see how your company handles customer service issues. Whenever there is a positive comment, make sure you thank your customer for it.

Occasionally a negative review of your business may show up on your page. Here are some tips on how to react appropriately:

* **Respond to the comment** – Respond to the negative review publicly, as other customers will judge your company's service based on interaction. This will enable everyone to see how you are willing to do what is necessary to ensure a positive outcome, and you genuinely care.

* **Contact the user in a private chat** – After responding publicly, also send the user a private message to understand more about what has happened. After you solve the customer's problem, ask them to review your service again.

* **No excuses** – Regardless of if you had objective reasons for failing on quality or service, don't use it as an excuse to the customer. Instead, explain to them how this is not your usual pattern of behavior and make sure they understand they are important to you.

* **Contact information** – Always give the customer your direct contact information so they feel you are interacting

with them on a personal level, and the customer will revert directly instead of publicly until their satisfaction is restored.

* **Feedback application** – Use the customer's feedback and inform whoever is responsible in your company for that failure. Take any actions possible to prevent this problem from occurring again.

Deleting negative reviews or hiding them will result in more negativity because your non-satisfied customer will find other channels where they will post more negative reviews.

Social Listening

Retailers can conduct social media listening, which is paying attention to what your target customers are talking about in regards to your brand. This means monitoring social media to collect information on how to enhance customer satisfaction, and personalizing marketing campaigns.

Social media affects how retailers communicate with customers: Many customers prefer to communicate via social media. Customers will either send messages, or post information or questions publicly. Social media is a channel on which customers provide both positive and negative feedback about products or service levels. When a customer posts such feedback online, it will affect the opinions of other consumers. It is essential that retailers monitor, or "listen", what customers write about them on social media, and quickly respond to both positive and negative feedback. When you respond immediately to a customer on social media to solve their problem, it creates loyalty and improves the company's reputation.

Before social media came into existence, customers considered a retail business to be an impersonal entity. If consumers online connecting with your brand are mostly a particular demographic (for example, age of 35), then it's very likely that other consumers that associate with your brand will be that particular demographic too.

Bosting Appeal Through Social Media

To improve your social media appeal to customers, use what you know about your audience in the moments and events that matter most to them. Then use social media to participate in these moments to get the audience's attention and eventually show them products that are relevant to those moments. To keep their attention, manage a series of creative shopping posts about your products. Creating cultural connections, such as supporting a sports events or a book launch, is a great technique to employ.

Typical Retailer Mistakes When Using Social Media
The most common mistake that retailers make in regards to social media is not moving fast enough with the adoption of technology and the adoption of new trends, for example still only using posts instead of including stories on Instagram.

If your social media does not offer value to customers when you interact, then you will soon lose the opportunity for engagement and capturing the interest of the customer.

Chapter 11

STEP-BY-STEP GUIDE

*Marketing's job is never done. It's about perpetual motion.
We must continue to innovate every day.*

Beth Comstock

L ET'S GO THROUGH A STEP-BY-STEP example of a well-planned and executed digital content marketing transformation. We will use a very simplified model following the chapters of this book. The main purpose is to illustrate the basic process and principles involved in each step.

The main goal is to make your current marketing model more effective online by using the principles of content marketing. Content marketing should enable long-term success at a lower cost, while creating a community of followers who will become your loyal, satisfied customers. They will then be spreading positive word-of-mouth and do branding for you.

One of the most significant reasons to do organic content marketing well is that your efforts will create organic traffic, backlinks, and community engagement. This will increase your relevance, and with increased relevance the cost of paid ads decreases.

In this example, we'll cover the steps for:

* Creating your content marketing machine
* Bringing more organic traffic to your pages
* Convincing search engines that your business belongs on top of the search results

* Reducing the costs of paid ads by increasing the relevance of your webpages
* Managing social media so it's adapted to the Hook Model
* Communicating online in line with the best practices for online engagement
* Creating a Story Branding style of communication to share your company message better
* Creating Social Media accounts or updating existing for maximum effect
* Communicating on your Social Media accounts in a structured way

Naturally, the following summary of principles is merely a simplified model to serve as a reminder of all the steps that you need to take care of to create a successful content creation machine. The principles of improvement are the same no matter the size of your business, and they will drive you to a better future and profits.

REVIEWING CURRENT ONLINE MARKETING

Let's start by reviewing your current online marketing. Does it match with actions that are proven to deliver maximum results?

This part of the transformation is described in chapters 1 and 2. Please consult them for more detailed explanations of each step.

Answer the following questions:

1. **How does your brand look online?**
   * A brand is not merely an image of a company: a brand is what the company does, which means that brands are about actions instead of advertising.
   * The real differentiator of a successful brand is that it looks and feels consistent.
   * When you see a successful brand online, it will have many media types and channels where customers and prospects can interact (blogs, Facebook, Twitter, Pinterest, YouTube, Instagram, website, and potentially many others). All those

media types and channels are used by brands to showcase the values that they represent to the public.

2. **Is your online retail marketing offering customers value?**
   Content marketing in retail is about:
   * What your customers value.
   * What their life aspirations are and how your business helps them achieve their goals.
   * How you can help customers by providing them value, educating them, while also entertaining them.
   * Growth of your online sales is all about the audience, and if you can create the trust with your online audience that will ultimately be in high value if you have products to offer to them.

3. **Are you enabling customers to find you online?**
   * Customers can only find you if you publish content.
   * Enabling customers to find you online is the result of steady, consistent work, which is where most retailers fall down.
   * The point of content is that it creates a flow in the customer's mind, to convince them to trust you and eventually make a purchase.
   * Your content has the potential to bring a particular type of person to your e-commerce site and help them make a purchase.

4. **Do you depend on paid ads to bring traffic to all your channels and websites?**
   * When you pay for ads you are not really buying attention, you are really just renting it for a short time because ads are temporary. When you stop paying the rent, you stop getting attention.
   * Become what customers want to consume online. So instead of finding customers, they will find you.
   * Increasing organic traffic instead of paying for ads will bring you long-term, sustained traffic.

5. **Are you using the Hook model in your online actions to create loyal users?**
   * All retailers can use the Hook model to get consumers on board with their service and products. Once consumers are hooked, there is less need for costly marketing and advertising.
   * Hooked consumers will advertise your business online by word-of-mouth.

REVIEWING CURRENT INTERNET TRAFFIC

This part of the transformation is described in chapter 3. Please consult it for more detailed explanations of each step.

Answer the following questions:

1. **What is the percentage of organic traffic arriving on your website?**
   * You can check this data in Google Analytics.
   * The most crucial difference in comparing paid to organic traffic is that organic traffic is free, and paid traffic is paid.
   * There are two ways to get traffic from search engines. Your website can be highly ranked in search results, or you can pay for ads (such as Google Ads) to place your ads on top of the organic results.
   * Organic traffic is the most important traffic that you can get to your website, for the simple reason that organic traffic is very targeted. When people type a query in a search engine, they have a specific intent, and if you can provide them a solution, then you might gain a new customer.

2. **How do you rank compared to competitors?**
   * The best and easiest way to check is to use the tool Alexa. com, for which you can get a free trial.
   * When you rank well due to your organic results, usually, it is long-lasting. When you invest money in organic positioning, then those results are extended over long

periods, while money for paid search traffic is spent over and over again.

* One of the most important factors, in deciding whether to invest in efforts to increase your organic ranking and positioning, is how the price of paid search traffic is determined.

3. **Are you working on essential factors for high ranking?**

* To rank better than competitor sites that are of the same quality as yours, you need to create authority. That can be accomplished by getting links from high-authority sites and building your brand while creating an audience that will engage with and amplify your content.

* Search engines confirm that quality content and links are two of the three most important ranking factors for SEO.

* One of the significant steps in SEO is to get links from other trustworthy sites.

* Building backlinks is a great tool to build your brand and promote the products or services you offer.

4. **Are you actively working on creating user interaction with your content?**

* When your content gets people talking, you are promoting what social media sites want in the first place, which is interaction and user engagement. For that, you will be handsomely rewarded by their algorithms. Algorithms track user interaction by measuring metrics like comments, likes, and shares.

* Consistency is critical for social media algorithms. For your audience to recognize your brand, you must be consistent. Being consistent in your social media brand allows you to grow audience engagement and reach, satisfying both users and algorithms.

STRUCTURING CONTENT CREATION

This part of the transformation is described in chapter 4. Please consult it for more detailed explanations of each step.

The key takeaways on structuring content creation are:

* It is advisable to start with one person that will work on creation and publishing content. After your operation grows you can assign more people to your content team.
* It is always possible to find a person that likes to create content instead of just being appointed to such a task.
* Get the essential software tools for content creation and consistent posting, such as social media calendar software.
* To keep your team aligned to company goals while ensuring everyone does their part, set up a good structure.
* The process of creating your content needs to be well organized and flexible, no matter if you are a small retailer or a big one. Only a strong structure will enable good content to be consistently created by a motivated team.
* Consistency is one of the key factors which search engines check to determine if you are relevant in the field in which you publish content.

CREATING A BRAND STORY

This part of the transformation is described in chapter 5. Please consult it for more detailed explanations of each step.

The key takeaways on creating a brand story are:

* Create stories and build the brand through stories, starting with your main company brand and reaching to each product or service that you offer.
* The customer is the only main character in the story that you tell.
* Brand or product is never the main character of a story. Your company, as a product supplier, is only a guide for a customer, who is on a journey to become a superstar with your help.

* Create a simple umbrella message following the Story Branding rules described in chapter 5.
* Create a list of fifteen–twenty sentences that you will use on your social media channels in the future. They should describe how your company is serving as a guide on customer journeys to have a better life.

Developing Content Ideas

This part of the transformation is described in chapter 6. Please consult it for more detailed explanations of each step.

The key takeaways on developing content ideas are:

* You have to generate content ideas without a break and keep idea generation smooth. It is essential to have a process in place.
* The role of content is driving a customer through the buyer journey, and it is an integral part of each stage.
* One of the most challenging issues you will face is churning out worthwhile content ideas, on a steady basis.

Writing Efficiently

This part of the transformation is described in chapter 7. Please consult it for more detailed explanations of each step.

The key takeaways on efficient writing are:

* Compelling content is relevant and useful to your readers. Your writing should speak in the language of a customer, on a customer level, and discuss problems that they have.
* To make users read your content it has to be helpful and useful. Only then will people connect with you.
* When you show your expertise to customers, positioning yourself as a guide, they will start to trust you.

CREATING MEDIA PLATFORMS

This part of the transformation is described in chapter 8. Please consult it for more detailed explanations of each step.

The key takeaways on creating media platforms are:

* Retailers can use their blogs to connect with people, get feedback, and provide personalized promotions.
* When you operate a "neutral" blog, which publishes independent reviews on the same or similar products on the market, then you have a chance to influence readers more than when you run the same blog on your webshop.
* People tend to follow advice on what to purchase from sites that are not connected with the seller.
* People will always tend to follow advice more from an independent newspaper-like webpage than just a blog post.
* Creating a set of blogs, without naming them "blogs", establishes a set of your own media platforms that can cover any area you desire, to engage and inform the public.
* Decide if you can operate a useful set of your own "blogs" on different subjects, covering all the main areas in which you do business.
* In case you operate a webshop, decide if you also need a separate brand page. A brand page can be useful to publish your own news and information about the company. Information from your brand page can be posted on your social media channels.

CREATING SOCIAL MEDIA PRESENCE

This part of the transformation is described in chapter 9. Please consult it for more detailed explanations of each step.

At *www.dariosipos.com/resources* you can find an infographic on the process of creating social media profiles and how to run them to achieve maximum effect, starting with the CEO and including each person in your company.

Involve management in becoming social media thought leaders, so they can promote the company online.

The key takeaways on creating social media presence are:

* Social media is a great channel for communication between customers and retailers. The right way of using social media is creating a community.

* Customers will love your product or service more if you add content that helps them. The younger generations have a particular affinity for social media platforms.

* Retailers can personalize the consumer experience by using social media. A significant number of retailers still think that social media is only a marketing and sales tool.

* Posting content too often or posting irrelevant content is the same as cold calling. Every fourth post could be something about the product, and three posts should only be about users and what makes them happy.

* At first, open the seven best social media channels for retailers: Facebook, Instagram, LinkedIn, Twitter, Pinterest, YouTube, and Google My Business.

* Contact information needs to be consistent across all platforms so search engine crawlers can connect it and know it is accurate.

* The most used and most popular social network of Google is currently Google My Business. As it is a business-related social network, it is immensely important for any retailer.

* Start publishing content based on the rules and principles described in this book.

* Create thought leaders online from your leaders and managers. They should have a strong presence and be active on a few platforms, ideally at least on LinkedIn and Twitter.

* When creating the online presence of employees, don't worry about company ranks and positions. Employees who love and know social media are rare, so you need to make them your social superstars who promote your brand online.

* Connect sincerely with everyone possible online. Search for journalists and other influencers and then connect with them too.

Promoting Content Efficiently

This part of the transformation is described in chapter 10. Please consult it for more detailed explanations of each step.

The key takeaways on promoting content efficiently are:

* Content promotion ensures that content reaches its targets. If the content which you create is going to bring you benefits, then you need to have people actually read it. Therefore, your content promotion plan is of the same value as your content production.

* Organic content promotion increases the visibility of your content and the efficiency of your marketing campaigns without spending money on ads.

* The highest results for your company will be achieved when you use paid promotion on your best performing organic content. So, bringing both types of promotions together will bring you the best results.

* Use the methods described in chapter 10, in the section Methodology of Promoting Retail Online, to form relationships with influencers which will uplift your brand engagement.

* To see if your posts and all your efforts are liked by your intended audience, it is crucial to measure and analyze the results of your campaigns.

The reason it seems that price is all your customers care about is that you haven't given them anything else to care about.

Seth Godin

THE INDUSTRIAL AGE WAS REPLACED by the social age, and companies refusing to adapt to the social age will disappear from the market. Reliance on paid media is already a thing of the past, now non-paid media is the way forward.

To achieve success online, it is best to integrate your company's existence into all social media channels, platforms, and paid media. The future of marketing lies in being able to acquire and read big data that will identify, target, and engage customers. If you wish to survive in an ever-changing media arena, you need to live and experience it.

The old models of advertising and marketing are no longer valid because they are out of sync with the new digital world. Many CEOs tend to outsource their digital marketing because they do not trust their team. Instead, a better way is to focus on bringing content marketing knowledge to the company by educating employees.

When going through your content marketing journey prioritize and plan, then start small and grow bigger quickly.

Customer retention matters more than customer acquisition. Digital technology offers an opportunity to convert your clients to brand ambassadors. Upselling, cross-selling, and requesting referrals will turn your existing customers to brand ambassadors.

Congratulations on completing the chapters of this book. You have moved forward, transforming your retail business to have your own in-house digital marketing agency.

You are now ready to: start, manage, and grow a content process for your retail business.

At *www.dariosipos.com/resources* you can find all the graphical guides mentioned in this book and additional resources.

The next steps are to continue building and implementing your plan, staying consistent. Regularly search for new ideas that could be valuable to your audience. Content will enable you to start a relationship with your audience, and assure them you are on their side as a guide to a better life.

Do you want to continue your content marketing journey? I would love to continue growing with you, so feel free to reach out to me on social networks, and be sure to check my page *www.dariosipos.com* for content that will help you in your growth.

Together we can transform how your business functions, so you are an influential presence and voice on the Internet that people will trust and listen to above all others.

Sincerely,
Dario Sipos

A/B testing	A method in marketing research where variables in a controlled scenario are changed and the ensuing alternate strategies tested in order to improve the effectiveness of the final marketing strategy.
Ad blocking	The blocking of web advertisements
B2B	Businesses that sell products or provides services to other businesses.
B2C	Businesses that sell products or provides services to the end-user consumers.
Banner ad	A graphical web advertising unit
Blog	A frequent, chronological publication of personal thoughts and web links.
Bounce rate	In web analytics the percentage of visitors who leave after viewing a single page.
Call to action (CTA)	The part of a marketing message that attempts to persuade a person to perform a desired action.
Click-through-rate (CTR)	The average number of click-throughs per hundred ad impressions, expressed as a percentage.
Conversion rate	The percentage of visitors who take a desired action.
Cookie	Information stored on a user's computer by a website so preferences are remembered for future requests.
Cost per click (CPC)	The cost, or cost-equivalent, paid per click-through.

Customer acquisition cost	The cost associated with acquiring a new customer.
Description tag	A html tag used by web page authors to provide a description for search engine listings.
Domain name	The location of an entity on the internet.
Flash	Multimedia technology that allows lots of interactivity to fit in a relatively small file size.
Forum	An online community where visitors may read and post topics of common interest.
Geo-targeting	A method of detecting a website visitor's location to serve location-based content or advertisements.
Inbound link	A link from a site outside of your site.
Inbound marketing	A marketing model whose sales performance relies on the initiative of its client base to find and purchase a product.
JavaScript	A scripting language used to create interactive websites.
Keyword	A word used in performing a search.
Keyword research	The search for keywords related to your website, and the analysis of which ones yield the highest return on investment (ROI).
Link building	The process of increasing the number of inbound links to a website in a way that will increase search engine rankings.
Link popularity	A measure of the quantity and quality of sites that link to your site.
Marketing automation	The use of software to automate repetitive tasks related to marketing activities and connect different parts of the marketing funnel.
Marketing plan	The part of the business plan outlining the marketing strategy for a product or service.
Meta tags	Tags to describe various aspects about a web page.

Organic search	The unpaid entries in a search engine results page that were derived based on their contents' relevance to the keyword query.
Outbound link	A link to a site outside of your site.
Pop-up ad	An ad that displays in a new browser window.
Return on investment (ROI)	The ratio of profits (or losses) to the amount invested.
Search engine	A program that indexes documents, then attempts to match documents relevant to the users' search requests.
Search engine optimization (SEO)	The process of choosing targeted keyword phrases related to a site, and ensuring that the site places well when those keyword phrases are part of a web search.
Search retargeting	The use of a site visitor's search history as a basis for the ads that the visitor will see.
SERP	Shorthand for a page of search engine results, typically the first page of organic listings.
Social networking	The process of creating, building, and nurturing virtual communities and relationships between people online.
Spam	Inappropriate commercial message of extremely low value.
URL	The location of a resource on the internet.
Vlog	A blog that publishes video content.
Website traffic	The number of visitors and visits a website receives.
Word-of-mouth marketing	A marketing method that relies on casual social interactions to promote a product.

TOOLS

Analytics
SEMRush (*www.semrush.com*):
Internet analytics tool

MOZ (*www.moz.com*):
Internet analytics tool

Alexa (*www.alexa.com*):
Internet analytics tool

SimilarWeb (*www.similarweb.com*):
Internet analytics tool

Google Data Studio (*datastudio.google.com*):
A tool from Google that lets users make custom reports with data from

Google Trends (*trends.google.com*):
Internet analytics tool

Google's marketing services and external sources.

Social Media Calendar Software
Buffer (*www.buffer.com*)

Hootsuite (*www.hootsuite.com*)

Graphics Editing Online Software
Pablo by Buffer (*pablo.buffer.com*)

Canva (*canva.com*)

Asset Depositories
ThemeForest (*www.themeforest.net*):
Largest depository of WordPress Themes

Promo (*promo.com*):
Largest depository of promotional videos

News and PR
PRunderground (*www.prunderground.com*):
Affordable Online Press Release distribution service to Google News, social media, and 100+ news and TV websites

Right Relevance (*www.rightrelevance.com*):
Aggregator of news for use in content creation

RESOURCES AND FURTHER READING

Nir Eyal with Ryan Hoover. *Hooked: How to Build Habit-Forming Products*. Portfolio Penguin, 2014.

Donald Miller. *Building a Story Brand: Clarify your message so customers will listen*. Harper Collins Leadership, 2017.

'The Converged Media Imperative: How Brands Must Combine Paid, Owned & Earned Media'. Altimeter Group, 2012.

HubSpot.com Inbound Marketing Resources (*blog.hubspot.com*)

Dario Sipos website (*www.dariosipos.com*): Downloadable Infographics and other useful marketing material

www.ingramcontent.com/pod-product-compliance
Lightning Source LLC
Chambersburg PA
CBHW071155130726
47998CB00002B/516